What is Chakra Healing

How to open your Heart Chakra

By

Nick Zanetti

This book is dedicated to my amazing mother Nadia.
She taught me how to be a decent human being

Table of Contents

A word from the author

The Heart. The centre of life that donates oxygen and energy all around our bodies; home of the *Anahata, or **the Heart Chakra**,* and the trunk of our Tree of Life.

There is hardly a Chakra that holds the same complexity and importance as your Heart Chakra, perhaps with the exception of the mysterious Crown Chakra.

The healing of both aspects of your Heart Chakra are vital for your happiness and your wellbeing in life, as they are essential for having healthy and rewarding relationships with fellow human beings.

It is my belief that if more people were to work on their Heart Chakra, most of the issues and injustices that we are currently seeing in the West could improve dramatically.

The main reason for this is that when a heart is open, it becomes accepting of others because an open Heart can see that we are all the same, a small fraction of the same bigger entity that we can call the Universe, Nature, Energy or God.

I leave up to you to decide what to call this eternal aspect that connects all the living and unliving things, it is important in this book to understand that your Heart Chakra can make you FEEL this connection with others.

It is a feeling of unity, of oneness and interconnectedness with all life and everything around you.

When the Heart Chakra is blown open, the feeling is so overwhelming that most people start to cry tears of joy. It is a feeling a total relief, of total safety because deep inside you can FEEL that we are immortal, we are NEVER alone as we are part of something MUCH bigger than us, something that connects everything and does NOT end when our physical life ends.

A blown-open Heart Chakra creates an incredible feeling of elation and complete freedom, but it is also very demanding on the body and this is the reason why it usually never lasts for more than a day or two, that would be too demanding on the body.

What if you could awaken that feeling at command, though?

What if you were able to go inside your Heart and let its energy flow when you want it to?

Perhaps during a beautiful day with your significant other?

Maybe during the wedding of your best friend or even during a spirituality festival?

These are some of the aspects that I will address in this fourth, but second, book of the *What is Chakra Healing* series.

And now you may be confused, how is this book both the second and the fourth book of the series?

Let me shed some light on this aspect the first book I published in the *What is Chakra Healing* series was an introduction to the seven Chakras of the body.

In that book I explained the basics of how to open your Chakras and as you may have seen in that book, the Heart plays a major role in aligning Chakras.

Opening your Heart is such an important part of the balancing of the Chakras.

Let me now tell you precisely what you will find in this book:

- What is your Heart Chakra or the Love Chakra?
- The two aspects of the Heart Chakra: universal love, and self-love
- Why the Heart Chakra is NOT just the Green Chakra
- How to open your Heart Chakra
- 3 important differences between romantic love and sexual love
- Signs and symptoms of an unbalanced Heart Chakra and what to do about that in a practical, step-by-step approach
- What stones, crystals, essential oils, and energetic frequencies support and help both aspects of your Heart Chakra

- How to forgive yourself and your past, and start a fresh life based on true love
- How to overcome the fear of loving someone after you were hurt in the past
- How to use balancing inner journeys to heal your Heart
- Master the skill of going inside your inner world to heal your Chakras via guided visualisations
- Participate in a seven-day healing quest to awaken your Heart and balance your life

If you are as excited as I am to walk down this path, let us now begin!

Introduction

Have you ever felt stuck in your life, incapable of enjoying what was going on around you, even if you could not pinpoint the reason for that?

Often the feeling of being stuck, or the feeling that the days around us have lost their colours and they are simply dull and grey, comes from a blocked Heart.

Your Heart Chakra is the centre of joy and when it is open, it can lead you to some of the most memorable experiences that you will have as a human being.

At the same time, a damaged or closed Heart is one of the most saddening experiences for a human being.

You see your Heart governs your relationships, and if your relationships are shallow, that's a sign that the Heart needs to be balanced.

If you think that most people in the world are worthless, and that there are a lot of people ready to scam you and take advantage of you, that's another sign that your Heart needs healing.

At the same time, though, if you are constantly just helping others and you are not taking time for yourself, that's another sign that your Heart needs balance.

This is what this Heart Chakra book will be about: a practical step-by-step experience to balance your Heart, heal and open your Heart Chakra.

As I have explained in my previous books, this *What is Chakra Healing* series will be focused on the practical experience of following some guided inner journeys to specifically work on both aspects of your Heart.

On the one hand, we shall work on the Green Chakra, the aspect of your Heart responsible for universal love and acceptance.

At the same time, we will work on the less known aspect, self-love, which is commanded by the Pink aspect of your Heart Chakra.

If you are here looking for a long and, in my opinion pointless, encyclopaedia on the Chakras like many of the quack gurus out there propose then this is NOT the book for you.

I do not find it useful, in any way, to spend too much time talking, collecting information and using your brain when it comes to the mastery of your Chakras; I am all about the experience and the actual following of the daily practice I will teach you.

My whole message is for you to do something practical to feel your Heart opening. An action plan that you can follow, with a daily practice which will teach you how to balance the two aspects of your Heart.

No flourishes or embellishments here, this is a book of action and empowerment!

This is the deal, plain and simple:

- **Part One** is all about the Chakra info. I will tell you about the Heart Chakra and will explain both aspects of the Heart

- I will analyse the importance of the Green aspect of the Chakra and its impact on your life
- I will do the same for the Pink aspect of the Chakra and discuss the importance of balancing them both.
- I will also offer some ideas regarding stones, crystals, music, and essential oils that will work on the aspects of your Heart.
- I will focus on THE ENERGETICS of the Chakra rather than the physical manifestations of it. This means I will not discuss physical symptoms or illnesses that are sometimes linked to the Love Chakra, as I found them to be an unreliable parameter and in the ultimate analysis not really useful.
- Then we will go onto **Part Two**, and this part of the book is skippable if you have already read my first *What is Chakra Healing* book.
- In Part Two I will explain to you the foundations of using inner journeys to balance the Chakras and I will guide you through the evaluation process.

Part Three is the most important part of the book and is the critical centre of my thesis. This is where I will guide you through seven inner journeys to learn about your Heart Chakra opening.

The first three journeys will be dedicated to the Green Chakra, the universal love aspect.

- The second three journeys will be dedicated to the Pink aspects of the Chakra, the self-love aspect.

- And the final journey will tie everything together and will specifically teach how to open your Heart Chakra and how to find true balance in it.

Now that I have made it clear what this book is and is NOT about, we are ready to start with chapter one, the Chakra definition and explanation.

Chapter 1
What is Chakra Healing: The Heart Chakra

Your Heart Chakra is the central energy centre of the systems of the body.

This is the fourth Chakra of the body and its Sanskrit name is *Anahata*. The word has several possible meanings and translations from this ancient language.

The ones that are most used in translation are:

- Unhurt
- Unbeaten
- Unstruck

Let's pause a moment to try and understand the meaning of this. These words are used to empathise the idea that once the Chakra is balanced you can become capable of forgiving your past and heal your spiritual wounds.

This interpretation is not incorrect; it is in fact true that a balanced Heart will help you to heal your spiritual wounds and guide you into being reborn into a new, stronger human being.

But the translation I agree the most with is actually quite different and it goes like this:

"the sound produced without touching two parts"

Now this translation may seem difficult to understand at first glance but bear with me and you will see why I really think this is the real way of addressing your Heart Chakra.

There is so much to learn from ancient cultures when it comes to the energetics and the spirituality of the world. Remember that a lot of these concepts come from a time where the world was much slower and there was almost no technology available and thus humans were more prone to sit and be still, be present in the moment.

Let's see why the words: "the sound produced without touching two parts" are so essential in your path of mastering the flow of energy through your Chakras.

Your Heart Chakra is the fourth, out of seven, of the Chakras of the body.

It is literally the energy at the centre of the two different systems of your body's Chakras.

Let me give you an explanation about this.

Your first three Chakras, the Root, Sacral and Solar Plexus Chakra, are called the Physical Chakras, or the Chakras of the Earth.

These are the three Chakras that you will find buried underground in your Tree of Life (more on this in Parts Two and Three).

The last three Chakras of the body, the Throat Chakra, the Third Eye and the Crown Chakra are called Spiritual Chakras, or Chakras of the Sky and you will find them in the branches of the Tree of Life (also explained in Parts Two and Three).

Your Heart is the bridge that connects these two words that DO NOT touch but are still part of the same structure: you.

With your Heart being the mediator between the lower earthly energies and the higher spiritual energies, I find it appropriate to translate its name with "the sound produced without touching two parts".

This is especially true because the frequencies of the Heart are used to send love to all the other Chakras to rebalance and heal them.

This is also the reason why this book is the second book in this *What is Chakra Healing* series, as it is of paramount importance for you to learn how to use the love coming from your Heart to balance all the aspects of your being.

Let us now go deeper and start to see more about this wonderful energy centre.

This Chakra is really the place where you can FEEL the sense of oneness and interconnectedness with all life, with God, The Universe, Nature and everything around you.

I am emphasising the word FEEL, rather than SEE because this is exactly how an open Heart works.

It gives you the feeling that the world is completely connected and that humans and all forms of life are also connected.

This is something that YOU CAN FEEL inside when you experience it.

This is a different experience compared to the awakening of your Sixth Chakra, your Third Eye.

This is because your Third Eye can SEE the truth about the world and the universe itself and when that happens you can look around and completely see the patterns of synchronicity of the beautiful world we are a part of.

For you to be able to do so though, you need to be able to open your Heart first, because this sense of feeling precedes the sense of seeing.

Think about a baby who hasn't been born yet: it has been demonstrated time and time again that a baby can FEEL his or her mother even with his eyes closed, even before the eyes are actually fully formed.

This is because the two Hearts, mother's and baby's, are connected and they are vibrating in unison.

This is the FEELING of oneness given by an open Heart.

To remain in the same example, if you have ever been fortunate enough to observe the way a baby looks at his or her mother, you would have observed the experience of oneness through the third eye of the baby, where he is able to SEE that we are all the same.

I know this may be a bit difficult for you to understand right now, but bear with me because in Part Three, during your practical training you will be able to feel what an open Heart feels like and I can promise you, it will be a life changing experience.

Going back to your Heart, consider that this energy centre is all about achieving unity, compassion and unconditional love.

This is the kind of love that is different from the more sexual type of love that is commanded by the Sacral Chakra.

Let me give a couple of examples to clarify this concept.

I would like you to think about a person you had a satisfying relationship with.

This relationship needs to be both a romantic and a sexual relationship for the example to make sense to you.

Now picture in your head a moment in your relationship where you were feeling extremely attracted to your special person.

You wanted to be with that person, you wanted to kiss that person and spend intimate time together.

That kind of sensual love where the physicality is important and there is an element of desire is the kind of love that belongs to your Sacral Chakra.

This Chakra is one of the Physical Chakras and as such, it commands physical situations like arousal and the desire to be together.

Now picture another moment during the relationship with this special person; perhaps a moment where the person was not with you and you were thinking about them.

Perhaps you were thinking about your next date, or how much you were missing them.

Now this type of love, which does not have an element of lust and desire, is the kind of love that comes from the Heart Chakra.

And depending how high the frequency of this love goes; you may even have experienced the strongest type of love that your Heart Chakra can give you: unconditional love.

This is the type of love that does not require you to feel any sort of attachment to the person you love, you love the person regardless of their choices and you just want the best for them.

This is an incredibly powerful type of love, like the love that caring parents may experience for their children where they will do anything in their power to protect them and make them happy.

Unfortunately, this type, as we will see later in the book, needs to be perfectly balanced by self-love, or it can become detrimental to the person.

Imagine a relationship where one of the elements of the couple are always trying their best to put the interest of their significant one ahead of themselves and imagine if this is taken to the extreme. This is when a person is essentially sacrificing him or herself for the couple and this is, obviously, not only potentially hazardous to the health and wellbeing of the person, but it is also strongly unbalanced for the relationship itself.

As you can see, the mastery of the Heart is a complex and exciting mission and through the pages of the book I will guide you to achieve exactly this.

For now, I shall see you in the next chapter.

Chapter 2
The Heart Chakra, The Green Chakra

Let us now consider the most common aspect of the Heart Chakra, the green part of it.

The Heart Chakra is the fourth Chakra of the body and it is located at the centre of your chest where your Heart is, and it can be found in the trunk of your Tree of Life when you are journeying.

This is the bridge between the Chakras of the Earth, the first three located underground in your Tree of Life and the Chakras of the Sky, located in the branches of the Tree of Life.

It is commonly associated with a gland of your body called the thymus.

This is an interesting gland as it is responsible for an incredibly important aspect of your immune system.

Have you ever heard of a set of cells in your immune system called lymphocytes?

If you haven't, these are the cells in charge of protecting you against threat by triggering a very powerful branch of your immunity called adaptive immunity.

Lymphocytes are made in the bone marrow, but lymphocytes T mature in the thymus to become active and ready to defend you.

It goes without saying that a healthy Heart Chakra is of paramount importance for your health and wellbeing and in the rest of this book I will teach you how do achieve this goal.

Let me be very clear now though, this book is designed for you to ACT and commit to following the practice in Part Three.

This is a crucial aspect of my message as there are too many quack gurus out there who are trying to repackage the same information time and time again without giving readers a practical solution to balance their Heart.

This is EXACTLY what I will teach you in Part Three, BUT for you to be able to achieve this balance, you will need to be brave and go through the practice exactly as it is designed.

This will be an emotional moment for you as I will ask you to face your inner fears, but this is also the only way out of a damaged Heart Chakra.

Love and self-love are behind the gripping fear that you may have experienced and that you will need to face later in the book.

The Heart Chakra is, alongside your Sacral and Third eye, a Yin type of Chakra.

This means that the type of energy, called Ki or Qi, present in this Chakra is a type of accepting energy empowered by acceptance and forgiveness.

When the flow of this energy is balanced, you will feel at peace with yourself and the world around you and if you manage to reach the perfect balance, you will be at a stage of your life where meeting your Twin Flame or Soul Mate will be very probable.

Let us now see the signs of unbalance in the Chakra and the possible reasons why that was the case.

Overactive Green Chakra

As you will learn later, both the green and the pink aspect of the Heart Chakra needs to be in balance for the Heart Chakra to function properly.

Unfortunately, life puts this Chakra under a lot of strain so it is quite common to see people with an overactive Heart Chakra.

Let's list the signs now:

- The first sign is the CONTINUOUS putting the needs of others ahead of your needs. There is nothing wrong in being altruistic and putting other people before ourselves, this is actually a characteristic of a good leader who can help and keep his or her group united and strong. The issue here arises when this type of behaviour becomes extreme and you may start to make unhealthy choices in the name of love. This is a clear sign of an overactive Green Chakra.
- Another important warning sign is the loss of personal boundaries which may lead you to make some relationship "choices" that you end

up regretting. This usually happens when a person a person with a strong Heart Chakra but an underactive Root Chakra, meets a person with a strong Root Chakra. Often over the course of time, the person with the strong Root Chakra may start to influence the person with the overactive Heart who may lose some of their boundaries just to keep the love going.

- The third and final aspect that I want to cover here, which happened to me several times in my youth, is when the person you are in a relationship with becomes your entire world. This is once again a typical sign of an overactive Heart and underactive lower Chakras. There is nothing wrong in loving someone to the moon and back, this is actually healthy as people who love tend to experience more enjoyable lives, BUT you cannot lose your sense of identity and self-esteem just in the name of love. Your sense of identity as a unique human being is granted by your Solar Plexus Chakra. If this Chakra is too weak and your Heart Chakra is overblown, you may end up in a relationship where your significant other becomes "ALL YOUR WORLD" and this is unhealthy as relationships need to nurture all the people involved with them not only a fraction of the participants.

As you can see, it is all connected, each Chakra (even the ones that don't really seem to be as exciting as the Heart Chakra or the Third Eye) play an incredibly important role in your balance as a human being.

But it goes even deeper than this!

This dominance and hyperactivity of the green aspect of the Heart Chakra is not only caused by an imbalance of the lower Chakras, but it is also often associated with a weak mastery of the self-love, pink aspect of your Heart.

Both the green and the pink part of the Chakra need to be balanced for the Chakra to be in harmony. You will learn how to do so in Part Three during the guided journeys into the Heart.

Let us now look at something really common: the sign of a damaged or blocked Heart Chakra.

Underactive Green Chakra

I will now cover the signs of an underactive, blocked or damaged Heart Chakra.

This situation here is, in my experience, extremely common in people once they have been badly hurt in a relationship.

Consider how often this could happen during the lifespan of a human being and you may start to understand the importance of reaching this balance.

The truth of the matter is that the majority of human beings have experienced the sorrow of "a broken heart" at some stage of their life journey, and that may have led to a blocked Heart Chakra.

Let us now see the signs:

- The first sign of an underactive Heart Chakra is the difficulty of getting really close to anyone, at least romantically speaking. This has hardly anything to do with the other person/people in the relationship, but more with ourselves. Sometimes the damage is so severe that we don't even open up for the ideal person at the ideal time. This is largely due to the fact that once the Heart feels the sorrow of being shattered, it may take some time and effort for the Heart to trust and try once again. The good news here is that Hearts are brave and, with the right tools, your Heart will be able to open up and love once again. I will teach you how in Part Three.

- Another aspect of a closed Heart is the difficulty in sharing feelings and letting go in a relationship. When a person is in this scenario, you may feel that they are always tiptoeing around the topic of love and commitment and that they try to avoid discussing their feelings. A typical scenario is when you are dating someone, and you are not sure what your relationship actually is. Are you just dating? Are you boyfriend and girlfriend (or any combination)? Are you just seeing each other? If you have ever been in situation like this, you may have been going out with a person whose Heart Chakra was not ready for romantic love. Keep in mind that there is nothing wrong with it, simply accept that

28

this person may not be, for now, the right person to consider when thinking about a committed relationship.

- The final sign that I want to address here, is the difficulty in forgiving yourself or others. See, the green nature of the Heart when blown open is to be universally loving, everything and everyone becomes showered with love with a full-blown Heart Chakra. This is because this Chakra can feel the unity and oneness of every living being in the universe. Unfortunately, when the situation is the opposite and the Heart Chakra is blocked, forgiving may be a demanding or straight up impossible task.

For now, let us analyse some of the common reasons why the Green Chakra may become underactive:

1. You are still dwelling in the shadow of an ended relationship. This is an important steppingstone that you need to learn about as fast as possible. Your Heart contains Ki, your energy, your life force. Energy does not understand the concept of time, but it resonates with vibrations or

frequencies. If your mind stays in the past in a concluded relationship, your Heart will not be able to open up to a new one. Letting go of the past, is of paramount importance for the opening of your Heart.

2. You are afraid of being hurt and you are experiencing trust issues. This is huge! For the Heart to be balanced, courage is necessary. Hearts thrive when facing a challenge with bravery even when if it fails. Remember this, you do not need to win to balance your Heart. If you try and trust a person and you try loving that person and the person still ends up breaking up with you, you are still doing this right! This is because you are feeding your Heart with bravery and bravery leads to strong Heart.

3. And the final aspect that I want to cover here is holding on to the past or experiencing resentment. You may resent yourself or someone else, it does not matter, but resentment, vengeance and grudges are all emotions that keep you stuck in the past and your Heart Chakra cannot be healthy when lingering in the

past. The ONLY way out of this conundrum is by mastering forgiveness.

Amplifiers for the Heart Chakra

It is now time to discuss some amplifiers for the green part of your Heart Chakra and in this section, I will specifically cover crystals and stones, essential oils and frequencies that will support your Heart.

I will start with my favourite four stones/crystals for the green aspect of the Heart Chakra; there are many more than the ones described here, but these are the ones that I see giving the most CONSISTENT improvements to my clients.

Let me list them in order of usage, from the first one to use when you are starting to work on the green aspect, to the last one in the correct order:

1. Green aventurine: The first stone to use when working with your Green Chakra is green aventurine. This is a stone used for the activation of the Chakra and it is commonly used for 21 days at a time as the first stone for the green

31

energy. It does have a strong connection to the Earth, and it helps activating the Chakra by attracting the flow of Ki from the lower, Earth Chakras.

2. Green Jade: This stone is the second one that should be used in your path to influence the green aspect of the Chakra. It is commonly used for seven days straight and then worn every other day for seven more days. The importance of green jade for the Heart Chakra is the support of serenity and harmony of the Chakra. So, the aventurine helps in activating the Chakra and the green Jade helps its natural balancing.

3. Green calcite: This is the third stone to be used when working on the Green aspect and it is commonly used for 13 days after you have finished the cycle of the green jade. Its properties are to defend against negative vibrations and to stabilise the Chakra. There is also a second aspect of the stone, and the importance of this stone cannot be overstated, as you should wear it continuously also after the whole process of healing of the Chakra has been achieved as a

shield against negativity and as good charm when you start a new relationship.

4. Emerald: this precious stone is the last one to be used in process of the frequency healing of the Heart. It is usually worn for four days and four nights after you finished with the calcite and after these four days, it is common practice to go back to the calcite. Emeralds are stones of incredible power and their vibration calls to the Universe to release the power of universal and unconditional love from your Heart Chakra. It is common to experience a full-blown Heart Chakra in the days where you are wearing the emerald stone, if you follow the procedure illustrated.

The next topic that I want to cover is essential oils to stimulate the Heart Chakra.

My focus here is ONLY on the oils that I have tried and tested in journeys, meaning I have direct experience of them being able to support the practice of inner journeying. There are many different essential oils that can support this aspect of the

Chakra, but for the purpose of the inner journeys which I will teach you later, I found two oils to stand above all the others:

1. The first one is Pine essential oil, and this is also the oil that I would smell before the first three days of the practice in Part Three.
2. The second one is Neroli essential oil, this is also the oil that I would advise you to smell prior to the seventh guided journey in Part Three.

The final amplifier that I would like to discuss with you when it comes to your fourth Chakra are energetic frequencies and music for the Chakra.

Once again, I will relate specifically to what I found to be most EFFECTIVE when it comes to the practice of journeying and when it comes to the Heart Chakra I have two pieces of advice for the type of music to listen to when journeying.

The first one is the Heart Chakra Frequency which should be between 580 Hz and 639 Hz.

This is the spectrum of frequencies that I have tried and found to be the best when it comes to journeying via the tree trunk of the Tree of Life.

The second is a spectacular music video that I have found on YouTube and that is incredibly effective to vibrate at the right frequency of the green aspect of the Heart.

The YouTube video I am suggesting you is from a channel called Meditative Mind and the title of the video is extremely powerful Heart Chakra opening vibrations (1 hour version) and you can find it here

Either this video, or some sounds in the correct frequency range, will help dramatically in your journeys.

Chapter 3
The Pink Chakra or the Self-Love Chakra

Now that we have covered the green aspect of the Heart Chakra, we need to take a step back and discuss the little-known aspect of self-love and the Pink Chakra.

Self-love is a concept that is often tossed around a lot in the self-help community, although very few people follow what they preach.

This is especially common among very altruistic and spiritual people; this is mostly due to the fact that once you enter in the quest for learning more about yourself, it becomes very easy to awaken the green aspect of the Heart Chakra. Once that is awakened, if you do not pay attention, it is simple to become very altruistic following your Green Chakra.

This is very noble and, as I said before, you also need to learn from the pink aspect of your Chakra as it is impossible to be balanced and healthy in the long run if you don't open up this part of your Chakra.

So, even if it may seem to you a dreadful idea to spend time thinking about yourself, or putting yourself first in some situations, I am asking you to trust me on the matter as it is of paramount importance for the long term.

What I am asking you here is to just try, even if you think you do not deserve to be put first sometimes, even if it is outrageous for you, just follow through with the practice and see how it works for you.

Should you want to discuss your situation please do so in the Facebook group "Chakras Explained with Nick Zanetti".

Self-love is important to living well. It can have a profound influence on your relationships and who you decide to accept into your life.

There won't be space in your life for an abusive relationship if you develop self-love, you won't accept a working situation that diminishes you when you develop self-love.

This is a powerful tool to have at your disposal, and when it is combined with a strong Throat Chakra it can make you literally unstoppable!

Imagine a situation where you love yourself enough not to stand any abuse any longer, COMBINED with a powerful inner voice that commands you to speak your truth without any fear.

The most important, positive, world-changing leaders have this gift and see how much society has improved thanks to people who were not afraid of speaking the truth.

I will explore more about the Throat Chakra during the sixth book of this series which will be available soon.

With this explanation covered, let us now see the signs of an unbalanced Pink Chakra.

Overactive Self-Love Chakra

I want to start this part of the book by describing what you could notice when the Pink Chakra is overactive.

There is nothing inherently wrong with having a very active Pink Chakra, and I actually think that it is best for it to be overactive than underactive. That said, balance is found in the middle, when both aspects of the Heart are working in a balanced, harmonious way.

Let's see now the signs:

- The first thing that may make you suspect that a person has an overactive Pink Chakra is that they often wear a lot of pink and they tend to dress to impress even when they are not in a socially important situation. Let me clarify that there is nothing wrong in doing so, and I am far from judging people dressing well and wearing a lot of pink, I am just pointing out a sign that you may notice.

- Another thing that you may hear from a person with an overactive Pink Chakra is the consistent use of the world "I" and the continuous effort in making them the main topic of the conversation. Once again, there is nothing wrong in talking about yourself and expressing your feelings and ideas; this is actually something healthy and good for you! The problem with this comes when this idea is taken to the extreme and the person cannot see anything beyond themselves. I used to have a friend like this during my first year of university. I used to talk to him about my problems and insecurities, but he never even replied to me when I had done so. The only thing he did, was to twist the conversation towards things he wanted to talk about. An example of this was when I had just failed a university exam and was feeling upset about it. I would talk to him b he would change the topic quickly to something that was happening to him which, in his mind, was 100 times more serious than my situation. So, keep an open eye and if you spot this kind of behaviour in a person consider if you

40

want a relationship with someone who tends to put themselves first in the vast majority of the situations.

- The final sign that I want to discuss with you is when you spot someone hardly bending their rules and their choices to accommodate others. Keep in mind that there is a lot of power coming from standing your ground and taking powerful decisions. But there is also flexibility that needs to be involved! If someone is never taking a step towards accommodating another human being, that's a clear sign of the Pink Chakra being dominant over the green one. This will need to be toned down to achieve balance.

Underactive Pink Chakra

Let us now cover the three main signs that are easy to spot regarding a person having an underactive Self-Love Chakra.

- The first one is, as previously explained, when you feel that the needs of others should always be ahead of your own personal needs. It is very noble to put others ahead of yourself, but there must be balance in this process. If you realise that your decisions are always made to accommodate others and you are hardly taking care of yourself, it is now time to start developing this powerful self-love.

- Another sign is feeling guilty when you are doing something nice for yourself. This is a major problem that a lot of people experience. I cannot even recall the amount of times when while explaining a lifestyle plan to a client of mine during an holistic consultation, I can see and feel guilt in them when I am asking them to do something for themselves. Some people feel guilty for having to spend some money on their own health! And if you are experiencing this, you must change. It is right as a human being to be healthy and happy, no matter what you have believed so far.

- The final aspect I want to remark on here is the need of some people to feel inferior or abused in a relationship. This is one of the most severe signs of a weak Pink Chakra, alongside a weak

Root and Solar Plexus Chakra. I have seen this happening time and time again with really smart and talented people dating (apologies for the term) "scumbags". If this is you, you need to change this because a relationship where you are put in a position of inferiority, or you are taken advantage of, is just a terrible relationship for you and so you NEED to develop this powerful self-love and break those chains.

There are obviously other signs of this kind of situation, but in ultimate analysis they all boil down to the three categories I have just covered.

If you see yourself in any of those categories, do NOT worry and be grateful to the Universe for this opportunity that is happening to you.

The Universe brought you here, and you are exactly where you need to be. It is not random that you are reading this book here, you were guided here by the Ki flowing in your Chakras looking for balance and by the end of the book, you will have the tool to deal with the situation and develop your strong sense of self-love.

Amplifiers for your Pink Chakra

Let us now analyse what kind of stones, essential oils, and frequencies I have found to be the most effective ones when it come to the Pink aspect of the Heart Chakra.

Exactly like I did with the Green Chakra, I will give you advice from a position of what I have found to be THE MOST USEFUL amplifiers based on my experience and my work with thousands of clients during the course of my years as an holistic practitioner.

These explanations on the amplifiers are not designed to be an encyclopaedia on stones and oils for the Chakra, but they are rather a clear and concise guide on what works.

With that explanation out of the way, we are ready to start with the stones:

1. The first stone to use when it comes to supporting your Pink Chakra is Rose Quartz. This stone is the one to be used in the awakening of the Chakra and you can do so by wearing it for 11 days straight as you start your journey into self-love. Rose quartz teaches you the power of self-compassion and the strength of loving yourself despite any perceived flaws or imperfections. It is the stone with the strongest message of accepting your condition of a human being. Human beings are fallible, imperfect creatures and we ALL make mistakes. This is fine as it our nature as humans to make mistakes and this stone will vibrate in a harmonious way with your Pink Chakra until you will deeply accept this reality. To get the best frequency of the crystal, please buy a true rose quartz stone from Brazil.

2. The other stone that I have found to be really supportive in the second stage of the development of self-love is amazonite. This is a stone that needs to be used AFTER rose quartz has worked its magic as this stone will ONLY

help your Pink Chakra after the Chakra had been awakened by the quartz. This stone bridges the gap between the Pink Heart Chakra and the Throat Chakra. When the power of this stone is unleashed, its gentle yet decisive vibration will help you stand up for yourself. This is because the stone will empower your acceptance that you are an important human being by increasing your self-love, and at THE SAME TIME, it will also start the healing of your Throat Chakra. This will grant you the capacity of accepting your importance as a human and the strength to make your voice heard. Use this for at least 11 more days after using the Rose quartz.

Next in our list are the essential oils that I have seen work the best in supporting the pink aspect of the Heart Chakra.

This oil is called Heart Pink and it comes from an Irish company called Unicorn and you can find the product here or by simply Googling Heart Pink Unicorn essential oil.

This specific essential oil is a blend of Lavender, Mandarin and Rose in Jojoba oil.

Its frequency is perfectly calibrated to support a healthy and balanced Pink Chakra.

To close this chapter, I also want to discuss some music.

The frequency that I have personally found to be the most appropriate to listen to when journeying for the pink aspect of the Heart Chakra is the 528 Hz frequency.

This frequency is not usually designed for the Heart Chakra, although I have seen this specific number work time and time again.

If you want a specific video to listen to when doing the Pink Chakra journeys you can find it here, or simply go on YouTube and find a channel called Spirit Tribe Awakening and the video to watch is 3 hours and 8 minutes long and it is called: "Enhance self love Healing music 528 Hz". This is indeed powerful music you can use to support your venturing into the secrets of your inner world!

Chapter 4
Final remarks and ideas for Part One

This is the end of the theoretical information regarding Part One, the theoretical one, and we are now entering Parts Two and Three, the practical parts of this book.

If you have already read my *What is Chakra Healing* book, it will not be necessary for you to read Part Two.

Part Two is an introduction to the practice of journeying; it will help find your Tree of Life and all the other significant elements of the experience in Part Three.

It will also give you the instruments you need to understand more about yourself and your Chakras and it will finally contain the Chakra test.

This is a test where you will partake in an inner journey with the purpose of finding out what are the

Chakras that you need to work on the most. Once you know this, you will be able to work directly using the journeying practice to address the issue.

This specific book is about the Heart Chakra. The first book in the series introduces all the seven Chakras of the body and the remaining books in the series will cover the other six Chakras.

After Part Two, the final part of the book will guide you through seven different experiences to balance both aspects of your Heart Chakra.

The first three journeys will be related to the green aspect of the Chakra, this will be followed by a day off. It is important that you try to plan your commitments to be able to enjoy the fourth day of the practice as a day off. A moment in time where you will dedicate as much time as possible to showering yourself with love. Please do plan accordingly as this is of paramount importance.

After the shower of love practice, you will have three more days of journeys and these will be focused on the Pink Chakra. This is where I will teach the step-by-step process to develop self-love.

Finally, there will one last journey and this will be specifically around the balance of both aspects. Its purpose is to make sure that both the green and the pink part of the Chakra shine with the same intensity improving your balance and your experience of life.

Now this may seem all nice and shiny to you, but I need to be really blunt with you.

This book is a practical manual, and as you see from the division of the chapters, the practice IS THE MOST IMPORTANT PART!

The internet is already full of websites, books and videos that describe the Chakras in detail and most of them do NOT give people a real, field tested, step-by-step approach to balance their Chakras.

This is EXACTLY what I will teach you in Part Three.

Knowledge and endless discussions without practical steps to improve your quality of life within a reasonable amount of time are worthless.

What I am here to give you is something that works quickly and directly on the balance of the Chakras.

This is a one-week guide to work on one of the major Chakras of the body and I have laid out all the steps, in a beginner-friendly way, for you.

This book will also be available as an audiobook, should you prefer to listen to the guided visualisations rather than read them.

I am trying my best to give you EVERYTHING that you will need to achieve your goal of balancing your Chakras; BUT this will ONLY work if you are willing to take the time and effort to practice.

This means not just reading the guide or just trying it a couple of times and then procrastinating and never finishing the book.

This book WILL have a profound impact on you, BUT you need to be the one taking the practice seriously.

How do you know if you are, then?

Well, let us just say that we are going to go very deep into the Heart's Chakra journeys and, if you do this correctly, it will be a very emotional experience.

You can expect tears, fears and elation.

The experience WILL BE INTENSE, as we will need to release years of trapped energy into the Chakra and when this old energy will be released you can be absolutely sure you will feel it.

So, I am begging you to take the practice seriously, I have laid in front of you the path to heal your Heart. It is there as clear as day, but I cannot be the one walking the path for you.

You need to be the one deciding to take the practice seriously and go deep into your inner world and come out victorious.

I have complete faith in you!

Disclaimer on Meditation, Guided Visualizations, and Inner Journeys

Meditation, guided visualisations, and inner journeys are generally considered safe activities, especially at the beginner level. At this level, they are mainly an exercise in relaxation and concentration.

However, the advanced levels of meditation, guided visualisations, and inner journeys can require a willingness to use your powers of concentration to engage in self-study and examination. If you feel you might be uncomfortable engaging in this kind of self-examination, then I ask that you do not proceed beyond the beginner level until you feel secure and comfortable with proceeding further.

If you have a history of mental illness please consult your healthcare provider before learning meditation, guided visualisations, and inner journeys. This is not to say that these will be harmful to you, but it is safer to avoid the risk.

Please be aware that I make no claim to be any kind of psychologist, counsellor, or medical professional. Anything I say or write should be considered my own opinion, and not an expression of professional advice, or a prescription. You are entirely responsible for how you choose to understand, use, or misuse any of my writings or communications. I can accept no responsibility for any adverse effects, direct or indirect, that may result from your use of the information in this book, or in any of my communications.

Furthermore, I make no guarantees that any of the information or practices in this programme will function in any certain way for you. By using this programme, you agree that you use the information contained herein entirely at your own discretion.

All the meditations, guided visualisations, and inner journeys described in the book will require your focus and attention. They are, therefore, unsuitable when you are in a situation that already requires your attention, such as driving or operating machinery. Never practice the meditations, guided visualisations, or inner journeys while driving a car or operating machinery. Choose an environment that is quiet and safe.

Medical Disclaimer

This book is designed to provide helpful information on the subjects discussed, and the information herein is solely the opinion of the creator.

This book is not meant to be used —nor should it be used— to diagnose or treat any medical condition(s). This book is not intended as a substitute for medical advice.

For diagnosis or treatment of any medical problem, please consult a qualified healthcare practitioner.

No action or inaction should be taken based solely on the contents of this information; instead, readers should consult appropriate healthcare practitioners on any matter relating to their health and wellbeing.

The creator does not accept liability for any consequences arising from following the information in this product, when advice should have been sought from a suitably qualified healthcare practitioner.

You are strongly advised to speak with your healthcare practitioner before implementing any of the suggestions contained in this product.

References are provided for informational purposes only and do not constitute endorsement of any websites or other sources. Readers should be aware that the websites listed in this product may change.

Part Two

IMPORTANT: This part is covered in all of my *What is Chakra Healing* books. You can skip this part if you have read any another book of this series, as it will be redundant.

This part has been kept, even in the bundle version of the book to preserve its authenticity, feel free to skip it

Welcome to Part Two of the book. This is where all the theory that we have discussed in Part One will become real.

In these chapters you will "feel" for yourself the power of balancing your Chakras, and the profound impact that this may have on your day-to-day life.

As I mentioned during the introduction, this part of the book will be all about the practice of inner journeys.

This means that for you to be able to appreciate the benefits of the Chakra practice, you will need to invest fifteen to twenty minutes every day, for the next seven days.

This means that each balancing day will be dedicated to a specific aspect of the Chakra.

Each journey will start the process of balancing the Chakra, but in some cases more journeys will be needed to complete the process.

Now though, I would like you to pay attention to the following image of a tree – this is the Tree of Life, and it is a representation of the flow of Ki through your Chakras.

The first three of your Chakras – the Root, Sacral and Solar Plexus Chakras – are Chakras of the Earth. In this image of the tree, they will be below the ground.

Your Fourth Chakra is the Heart Chakra. This is the Chakra that bridges your physicality with your spirituality. In the image of the tree, the Heart Chakra will be the tree trunk.

Finally, we have the three Sky Chakras – your Throat Chakra, your Third Eye, and your Crown Chakra.

In the image of the tree, these three Chakras will be within the branches, extending into the air, towards the sky.

The Tree of Life

Over the course of the next seven days, I will ask you to visit different elements of the Tree of Life during your inner journeys.

You will start your journey from your Inner World and then proceed to work on the aspect of the Chakra of the day.

Don't worry if things feel difficult to grasp at the moment. For each of the seven journeys, I will give you a clear step-by-step guide, and I will take you through the process.

All I am asking is that you commit to take the time to do all of the journeys for seven days straight. No unplanned pauses or days off in the middle. I will also ask you to evaluate yourself before and after these journeys.

I will now begin by explaining the Chakra test, and the evaluation process.

Creating your Safe Place

In the next few pages, you shall begin your inner journey practice. For this, you need to find a place which will be your safe place.

Your safe place will be an area where you can safely practice the art of meditating and entering your inner world.

To create this, you will need a place where you are safe, and you know that you won't be interrupted during the exercise.

It is also really important that you choose a place where, if you fell asleep, you would be safe.

This is important because sometimes during the practice, or even at the end of the practice, you may fall asleep. For this reason, ONLY choose a place where it would be safe to do so.

Here are some guidelines for creating your own safe place for practice:

1. Choose a place where you will have enough light to read, but not too much light to disturb you if you close your eyes. The explanations for the inner journeys are here in the book, meaning you will need to be able to refer to the book to check

the next step. A gentle source of light will be of great help to you here.

2. Choose a place that feels right for the practice. When you start this quest into your inner world, I suggest you find a place where it feels right to you to meditate. Eventually, the place that you have chosen will improve because the more you meditate in one place, the better the energy of that particular place will become.

3. Before your first journey, burn some white sage incense sticks for at least 10 minutes in the safe place you have chosen for your practice. White sage has a beautiful balancing effect on energy, and it clears the area of any residual energy stuck there. If you like the smell of sage, you can do this step before each journey.

4. Keep your safe place clutter under control. There is a reason why monks prefer to meditate in an uncluttered space, and it is the same reason why they try to live a minimalistic lifestyle. Too many things in your safe place will interfere with your practice and may distract you. Whenever

possible, keep the things around you to a minimum.

5. If possible, have at least one plant in your safe space. There is something inspiring about meditating close to a plant, and since the practice of the inner journeys will see you journeying into the Tree of Life, having a plant with you will help you dramatically. When it comes to house plants, everyone has their own taste so I would suggest you go with your intuition. If you would prefer a recommendation, then the plants that I have seen working well with this type of practice are lucky bamboo, the jade plant, and any bonsai trees.

6. Make your practice space comfortable at all levels. Consider this scenario: you are deep in your inner journey to heal your Heart Chakra, when you suddenly feel your body shivering because your room is too cold. Would that help your practice and deep release? Probably not. You want your safe place to be comfortable at all levels. The temperature should be not too hot, but also not too cold. The area should be

comfortable enough for you that you will not need to shift position every five minutes, but also not so comfortable that you fall asleep easily. Before starting your practice, sit in your safe place for five minutes and make a note if there is anything that you are not happy about. Correct any issues, and then begin your journey.

These were the basic tips regarding your safe place. Remember that the more you practice, the more you will charge your safe place with good energy, and the better it will become.

In addition, it will be very important for you to realise that the more you use your safe place, the more you will learn about it.

You may feel you want to add more elements to your safe place as you go along, and I would strongly encourage you to do so. Use your intuition to find what works the best for you.

For example, I have a 60-minute sand timer in front of me in my safe place, and I always watch the sand slowly falling down for at least one minute before I start my practice. I have found this to be incredibly relaxing for me, and it puts me in the perfect state of mind for the practice.

I encourage you to experiment and see what works best for you – find your personal touch. Remember – you are the person who is most in contact with your Chakras!

Chapter 5
The Journey Instructions

The purpose of this book is to support and balance your heart Chakras. However, I recognise that you may feel curious about discovering which of your Chakras require more of your help. With the Chakra test and the evaluation process described in this chapter, we shall do exactly that.

You must read, and accept the disclaimer for the guided meditations and visualisations that we will cover in this part of the book.

Please do this BEFORE starting the practice.

For this practice to be successful, I will need you to be comfortable in your safe place.

I have already described how to energetically create the space for your meditations, but now I would like to talk about safety and interruptions.

The place you will use for doing your journeys will need to be safe, and it should shield you from interruptions and noises.

It needs to be a place where you can put your total focus on the task ahead of you. Obviously, these exercises are not suitable if you are doing any activity that requires your full attention, such as driving or operating machinery.

Essentially, you will need to do this practice ONLY when you can lie down in bed, on a sofa, or an armchair. Somewhere you can do NOTHING else BUT the practice.

With this explanation out of the way I would like you to go your safe place, and remove all of the distractions from around you.

Remove the sounds from your phone – switch it off or place it on airplane mode and find your quiet balance.

In a moment I will ask you to visualise few things. If you are struggling with visualisations, you will need to work on that aspect as it is essential for the journeys.

I strongly advise you to read the instructions through at least once before starting the practice, and then read them again as you go through the exercise with me

This ensures that you will know what to expect next, and this will make the journey easier.

With the instructions clarified, let's dig deep into the Chakra test and your evaluation.

The Chakra Test

In this section of the book we are going to discuss a way for you to evaluate how you REALLY feel right now, at this stage of your life.

I will ask you to repeat the test at the end of the seven inner journeys for Chakra balancing, to evaluate yourself once again to see what has changed.

To start the test, I need you to go to your safe place. Please read ALL of the following instructions at least once, before reading them again as you go through the exercise.

Once you are comfortable in your safe place, I will ask you to close your eyes and take some deep breaths.

Take as many deep breaths as you need until you will start to feel calmer, and more in touch with yourself.

Now we will need to take the first step into your inner world.

With your eyes closed, I would like you to see yourself in nature.

It could be a garden, or it could be a forest, but you will need to be able to visualise trees and grass around you.

This garden is your inner world. In fact, it is the fragment of your inner world that you can now see.

As you become more comfortable here in your inner world, you will be able to visualise more aspects of it.

With each journey, your inner world may change and expand.

For now, I am just going to ask you to look around. I can assure you that EVERYTHING that I will ask you to see will be present, somewhere in your visualisation.

You may not be able to find it at first, but just keep exploring, and it will be there.

This is your inner world; you are the maker and master here, even if you may not be fully aware of that yet.

Once you feel comfortable in your inner garden, I would like you to look around – somewhere in your garden, there will be a tree.

It will be a different tree from all the other trees in your garden. It may be taller. It may be more colourful. It may be made of a different material.

You will recognise this tree, because when you look at it, you will feel that the tree FULLY belongs to you.

Look around and listen to your Heart, because your Tree of Life is somewhere in your garden.

Once you have found it, please walk back to the place in the garden where you originally saw yourself when you started your journey.

You will not be journeying to the Tree of Life today, but that will be the subject of the seven subsequent journeys. For now, I just wanted you to be able to find it with ease when you will begin your seven-day quest tomorrow.

I now need you to be brave. Look around in your inner world, and try to find a full-length mirror.

Look around, it is there somewhere. It may be large, or it may even be too small for it to reflect the entirety of your figure. Just remember that in this inner world, the laws of time and space do not apply, and you have total control over everything.

Once you have found the mirror, please approach it and look at your reflection.

This is the mirror of truth, and nothing can deceive you here. The mirror will ALWAYS show you the truth and obey your commands.

Look in the mirror now and ask the mirror to show you the first of your damaged Chakras.

When asked to do this, the mirror may show your damaged Chakra in your reflection.

Sometimes though, it just highlights an area, or gives you a feeling in one of your Chakras.

Do not worry if it doesn't work right away. Continue to ask the mirror until the truth has been revealed.

Remember you are asking for THE FIRST Chakra that is damaged. There may be more, but for now we just need to find this first one.

Trust your intuition and the power of the mirror of truth, and the Chakra will be revealed.

Once it has been revealed to you, physically put your hand on your body, close to the Chakra the mirror has shown you. You will feel that Chakra, and you will be able to understand if you are on the right Chakra or not.

This means that if the mirror is showing you your Heart Chakra, you will need to physically put a hand around your Heart area and feel your Chakra. You are in deep state now and you will be able to do so, trust me!

Trust your intuition and the universe. If you are at this point of the book, doing the exercise with me, you are at a stage of your life where you are ready for this.

Keep asking the mirror, and feeling your Chakra areas, until you know that you have found your first damaged Chakra.

Once you have found it, please take a moment to note it down. This will be your Chakra which will need the most healing in the following seven journeys.

You can now go back to the mirror and ask for the second Chakra that needs healing.

At this stage, two things may happen. Either the mirror will show you a different Chakra, or it won't show you anything.

If another Chakra needs healing, please proceed with the previous procedure, physically placing a hand around the Chakra and feeling it. Once you are confident that this is your second damaged Chakra, make a note of it.

Once again, repeat the exercise, this time asking for your third damaged Chakra, and making a note of it if there is one.

Continue asking the mirror for your next damaged Chakras, until the mirror shows you that there are no further damaged Chakras.

Make a note of all the damaged Chakras, as you may need to focus on these damaged Chakras throughout the following seven days of Chakra balancing.

Damaged Chakras:

1.

....

2.

....

3.

....

4.

....

5.

....

6.

....

7.

....

Once you have completed that stage of the exercise, you will need to move on to the evaluation step of your quest.

Take a moment to answer these questions, doing so in a mindful way. Remember that being able to assess your situation is one of the most valuable things that you can do for yourself.

The practice of sincere self-analysis is an important aspect of the healing of your Chakras. Spend five minutes on the following exercise, and answer all of the following questions:

1. **How do you feel right now, emotionally?**

   Rate your emotional health on a scale of 1 to 10 (with 1 being as bad as it can be, and 10 being the best it can be)

   ....

   ....

   ....

   ....

2. **How close are you to what you are looking for in life?**

   Please rate on a scale of 1 to 10 (with 1 being as far as you can be, and 10 being as close as you can be)

   ....

   ....

   ....

   ....

   And finally, what is it that you are looking for during this week of Chakra balancing?

   ....

   ....

   ....

   ....

Before you proceed with the next stage in the book, please ensure that you have completed these exercises.

If you have skipped these exercises, the next stage of your quest will not make sense. Please spend as much time as you need before starting with the Chakra balancing process.

Part Three

The Practice

Part Three
The Journeys

Day One - First journey to the tree trunk and the green lamp

I will now need to reach your safe space, switch off all the distractions around you and get comfortable.

You must read and accept the disclaimer for the guided meditations and visualisations that we will cover in this part of the book.

Please do this BEFORE starting the practice.

<u>There is another task to do before the practice and it requires some planning!</u>

<u>You shall proceed for the first three days with the guided meditations, and then on day four you will need to take a break and complete a different task which will require some time. It is of vital importance for this fourth task to happen in a day where you are free, ideally a day-off from work.</u>

So, if you are starting your practice on a Monday, please do plan ahead so you will have your Thursday (fourth day off)

It also helps to read the instructions of the journey through once before attempting it, to ensure that everything will go smoothly, and you will know clearly what to expect.

Once you are comfortable in your safe space, and after you have removed the sources of distractions such as phones and various notifications, I would like you to start to take some deep breaths and start to imagine that you are entering your inner world.

This is the same world you visited before when I asked to evaluate your Chakras in the mirror of truth.

Once you are in your inner world, I will now need you to walk towards your Tree of Life, this is the tree that I asked you to find in preparation for this journey here.

As I have previously told you, the rules of time, dimension and space do not really apply to your inner world, so once you are in the presence of the

Tree of Life, regardless of its size, you will be able to find everything that I will ask you to find.

If something is not there, just keep looking, everything you need is somewhere around, you just need to find it.

Now approach the Tree of Life. Look at it. Look around it. Appreciate how it looks, and how it feels.

For your first journey, you will need to travel to the position of the Heart Chakra in the Tree of Life.

This will be found in the tree trunk, so now please look around the tree trunk until you will be able to find an entry point.

Once the entry point has been found, you can start walking around inside the Tree of Life, looking for the room which hosts the power of your Green Chakra.

To recognise it, look for a room with a green door. That is the room you have to go in - this room will be the one that contains your Heart Chakra lamp.

If this is your first experience with inner journeying, (and from now on I will assume it is) you need to find the room with the green door.

As you approach this room, you will feel that your Heart starts to respond to the room, so get closer and touch the door.

Feel it in your Heart. This is the room which leads to the strengthening of your Chakra, and then open the door and go inside.

As you do so, you will be able to feel and see a green light which will surround you as you step in.

This is the light of your Heart, the source of the universal love and after you have enjoyed it for a few moments, I will need you to look around and find the source of this in the form of a green lamp.

This green lamp holds the energy of your Heart Chakra, please spend a bit of time observing it.

Is it rusty? Perhaps dirty? Does it require some repairing?

Chances are that if you are here taking this journey, something in the past may have hurt or blocked your Heart Chakra.

That damage will be visible on the lamp itself, and our purpose for the first three journeys of this week is to rejuvenate and repair your lamp and, in doing so, you will heal the wounds of the past and get ready for a new and exciting future.

I am afraid though, that in order to do so, you will need to go through an ordeal and pass a test that may be difficult to face.

This quest will hold the power of the healing of your Heart, so you need to be brave and trust the process.

I will be with you during this journey, whenever you need something just refer back to the book which will guide you in your endeavour.

Should you need further guidance, please join our private Facebook group called *"Chakras Explained with Nick Zanetti"* and seek further guidance there.

Always remember though, that this is your inner world and you are the master and maker of this world and you have TOTAL power over everything in here.

I will now need you to be brave and set some of the groundwork for the following journeys.

First of all, I need you to hold up your Green Chakra lamp and look around the room.

You will be able to see two further doors, one door is a nice relaxing pink door and it will be the destination of your last three journeys.

The other door is a bit more demanding, and it is a dark black door that leads to a place of challenge.

That dark door leads to the place that you will need to explore tomorrow, and it will lead to an adversary.

That will be the obstacle that you will need to overcome for you to be able to heal your Heart.

It will be an intense and emotional journey and you also need to remember that there is no reason for you to be scared.

The universe is with you. It believes in you, and so you will be victorious. Remember that the path of the Heart is a path that is enshrined in bravery. A brave Heart is a healthy, strong Heart and tomorrow you will show the universe your bravery. Once you will do so, a new path will open up for you. In that new path you will find the infinite source of universal love and that source will heal your Heart, vanquishing the damages and the blockages from the past.

For now, I just need you to spend a couple of minutes with your green lamp, really analyse it and hold it to your Heart. As you do so, you will be able to feel that you are vibrating at the same frequency as the lamp.

Feel that you are one with the lamp and one with the universe. Take some deep breaths and, as you do so, feel the energy of the lamp.

You are now starting to realise the secret of the Heart: a sense of oneness with everything around you, and as the days will progress you will be able to accept this more and more. As your Heart Chakra opens up, the love of the universe will flow towards you, transforming all of your existence.

BUT to do so you will need to complete your ordeal, and that will be the task for tomorrow.

Before I let you go and rest though, I will need you to do something brave for me. This is an important task, as it will prepare you for tomorrow by making everything easier.

So, while still holding your green lamp, you need to go and face the dark door which leads to the adversary.

Stand in front of the door but do not try to enter just yet. That is the task for tomorrow.

I need you to be prepared for tomorrow though, so as you face the black door, please answer the following questions.

You will need to answer from your Heart not your head, and holding your lamp close to the Heart will guide you in this part of the journey:

Who is the person that you will meet on the other side of this dark door?

....

....

....

....

Where is the damage on your Heart lamp caused by this person or the events related to this person?

....

....

....

....

And finally, would you consider forgiving this person?

....

....

....

....

Please answer these questions as honestly as you can as they will be preparing you for tomorrow's journey.

Also, since the practice is already working on your energies and your subconscious mind, you may even want to take some notes regarding any dreams that you may experience in the course of this week.

Just jot them down as you wake up, and re-read them for a few moments before the next journey you take.

If you want to have a practical workbook to take notes in, about the experience of the journeys, you can find purchase my *"What is Chakra Healing Chakra Info Workbook"* to assist you during this awakening process.

It is now time for you to go back to the physical world and take some rest after today's experience.

You have been very brave so far, and I am very proud of you. Tomorrow you will awaken the Heart of a hero.

Have a great rest of the day!

Journey 2
Vanquishing the adversary and finishing the ordeal

Here we are!

Welcome back to this crucial journey in your path to awaken the Heart of a hero.

Today we are going to journey deeper than even before and it will be a life changing experience.

As usual, for this to be successful I will need you to take some measures before we start.

I will now need to reach your safe space, switch off all the distractions around you and get comfortable.

It also helps to read the instructions of the journey, including the appendix, once before attempting it. This is to ensure that everything will go smoothly and you will know clearly what to expect.

Once you are comfortable in your safe space, and after you have removed the sources of distractions such as phones and various notifications, I would like you to start to take some deep breaths and start to imagine once again that you are entering your inner world.

Once you are in your inner world, I will now need you to walk towards your Tree of Life.

As I have previously told you, the rules of time, dimension and space do not really apply to your inner world, so once you are in the presence of the Tree of Life, regardless of its size, you will be able to find everything that I will ask you to find.

If something is not there, just keep looking. Everything you need is somewhere around, you just need to find it.

Now approach the Tree of Life. Look at it. Look around it. Appreciate how it looks, and how it feels.

Once there, just look around the Tree trunk to find the entry point which will lead you back to the room with the green door.

This entry point may differ from the previous one you used, and that is also OK.

Once you have gained entry to the Tree of Life, please look around for the room with the green door where your Heart lamp lies.

As you enter this room, let the green energy of the lamp envelop you and cuddle you.

Spend a couple of minutes just enjoying the light of your Heart and as you do so, go and collect your lamp and hold it in your hands.

For this next part, I will need you to look at the lamp and see how it has changed since yesterday.

See how your subconscious mind has already started the healing process, and it did so by starting to repair and improve your lamp.

Take a good look at it and notice all the differences compared to yesterday.

You are on a journey of self-discovery and empowerment; I want you to feel proud of what you have achieved so far!

With bravery in your Heart it is now time for you to face the black door and the adversary that lies behind it.

Hold your lamp in your right hand and with your left hand push the door open, if the door resists just move the lamp closer to the door and it will open up for you.

Remember you are the master and maker of this world and your will is unstoppable here.

Push the door open and get ready to enter the next part of your journey.

As you open the door, you will be presented with another space. It can be a place in nature. It can be in space. Often, it will be another room.

It does not matter what you see, just trust your Heart and enter this new space.

As you do so, you may start to feel fear or apprehension, and that is absolutely fine.

You are facing energetic blocks that may have been around for many, many years. It is fine to feel anxious or afraid.

See, the true Heart of a hero is not a Heart that is never afraid, but the Heart of someone who keeps going forward DESPITE the fear!

So, push through and enter this space. When you are inside, please look around until you find two chairs.

Somewhere in this space there are two identical chairs; one chair is empty, and one chair has a person sitting on it.

That is the person that you will need to face, once and for all, to close your ordeal and gain access to the healing energy of the universe.

Now, please go and sit in front of this person and let the trial begin.

You should already know who this person is from the previous journey.

If the person is not who you were expecting that is also OK. Trust yourself and the process.

Sit in front of the person and look the person in the eyes, even if this is hard.

Looking the person in the eye is a sign of bravery and bravery will heal your Heart.

If you are struggling just hug your green lamp and it will give you the strength you need.

You can do this, I have complete faith in you.

The universe brought you here, to this exact moment in time and space, and this is where you were meant to be. Look the person in the eyes and ask this question:

"What is it that you need to tell me?"

Pause and listen to the answer, and if nothing is said ask again:

"What is it that you need to tell me?"

And again, wait until the answer comes, and it will.

Listen to what that person has to say. If you feel fear, sadness, or any other emotion arise just hug your lamp and let your Heart help you.

Remember the energy from your Heart is the energy of love and love can heal any wound. Let the energy from your Heart pour into you, and keep listening to the person standing in front of you.

Once you have received the first answer, you will need to look the person in the eyes once again and ask:

"Is there anything else that you need to tell me?"

They may or they may not have something more to tell you.

Just listen without judgement to what that person has to say.

Take all the time you need here. Keep asking until the person has nothing else to say.

Give them one last chance to communicate with you because for the next stage, we will remove their influence once and for all.

Once this person has finished telling you what they had to say, you will need to enter into the final phase of the practice.

This is the moment where you will need to open your Heart and forgive the person in front of you, no matter how horrible the things they said were.

You see, forgiving is the most important gift of the Heart and you need to do if you want your Heart Chakra to be in balance.

I know it may be difficult for you, I know it can be really hard to forgive someone who hurt you, but holding on to that grudge in your Heart is even more detrimental for you and it will be the reason why your Heart will not be fully healed.

Be brave now, move your lamp close to your Heart and look the person in the eyes and with real honesty tell them:

"I forgive you for what happened in the past and now you need to leave this place once and for all."

Look the person in the eyes when you do so, and let your lamp burn brighter.

Accept the gift of forgiveness in your Heart and repeat once again:

"I forgive you for what happened in the past and now you need to leave this place once and for all."

Do this with truth in your Heart as it is time to let go, this person cannot poison you anymore, let the person go.

"I forgive you for what happened in the past and now you need to leave this place once and for all."

And with the strongest conviction that you can muster do it one last time:

"I forgive you for what happened in the past and now you need to leave this place once and for all."

And as you do so, you will see that the person and the chair will start to disappear from this space until they are no more...

Let them go. Say goodbye and, as you do so, I want you to feel this heavy weight lifting from your Heart once and for all.

Because the gift of a forgiving and accepting Heart is freedom, and freedom is earned after an ordeal. You have just passed your ordeal, and it is now time for you to rest.

I need you to take the next 20 minutes off, you need to rest a little longer.

Take this time off and rest. You have been brave, so let the universe heal you now as you deserved it.

And after this well-deserved rest, please come back to the book as I have few more things to tell you.

Now rest my brave hero!

Appendix to the second journey

OK, now that you have rested for a while after that challenging experience, I have some things to tell you regarding this kind of journeying.

First of all, it is important to realise that when it comes to the healing the Heart, the sentiment of forgiveness is of paramount importance.

You need to realise that the Heart Chakra perceives the world through the eyes of universal love, and for love to be universal it needs to be able to forgive no matter what the situation was.

An important notice here: forgiving does NOT mean that you shouldn't hold people accountable for their actions and act accordingly.

It is of paramount importance that you do that because if you do not do this, you will block a different Chakra like the Root or the Throat Chakra.

Forgiving the person/people in your inner journey means releasing a weight from your Heart. This is a cathartic experience for you.

This does NOT mean in any way, shape or form that you need to restart a relationship with someone who hurt you.

Forgiving means not carrying around grudge in your Heart any longer and when that has been accomplished, you will have the freedom to either get the person back into your life, or remove them completely.

Remember, as hard as it may be, this experience is for you, not them. Learn to forgive and let go, do not hold this weight in your Heart and be forever free to be who you really are.

Another important aspect that you may have experienced is that you may have seen yourself sitting on the chair in front of you.

It is possible that the person sitting there may have been you, or a part of you. This is also absolutely fine, if this was the case for you, you will need to work even harder in the last three journeys of this book, so that your self-love, your pink energy will help you heal your green one.

One last thing that I want to discuss with you related to this kind of journeys: as you may have noticed, I was very clear in the instructions for this quest.

I was guiding you specifically through the process of forgiving when vanquishing the enemy.

This was done intentionally, for the experience of the Heart Chakra is one of love and acceptance rather than power and victory.

You see, during the inner journeys when you are defeating and surpassing an adversary, you usually have two options:

1. You can either take the path of forgiveness
2. Or you can take the path of power and victory

An important reminder here: if you were educated in the West, you may feel that one is better than the other.

It is typically taught that forgiving is always the better option of the two; the truth of the matter is that this is not true!

See, the path of forgiveness is taught you by your left side of the body and it finds its expression in your Yin Chakras. These are: The Sacral Chakra, The Heart Chakra and the Third Eye.

At the same time, it is crucial to remind you that the path of power is equally important.

This path comes from your right side of the body and its strength lies in the Yang Chakras. These are the Root Chakra, the Solar Plexus Chakra and the Throat one.

These two aspects of your energy, your Ki or Qi are EQUALLY important and when you are journeying you often have the possibility of choosing the path that you desire.

This is mostly true, but it depends on what Chakra you are working on, and if it pertains to the Heart Chakra, choosing the path of power will not end up in a balanced Heart Chakra.

I know I put a lot on the table in this chapter here. If you want to learn more about the two aspects of your Ki and how they flow through your Chakras, I have a written a book, also available on Amazon, called *The Ki Quest Method*. That book is specifically designed to cover the two aspects of Ki and how to journey to balance them both.

I will close this appendix now, and I shall see you tomorrow for the next journey.

Tomorrow you will explore what lies beyond fear and what you will find will change your life forever.

Have a good rest and I will see you tomorrow for your third journey.

Journey 3
What lies beyond fear!

Welcome to your third day of practice and what a special day this will be!

First of all, let me congratulate you one more time as it was absolutely brave of you to have faced your inner fear yesterday and come back victorious.

Today is the day where you shall explore what lies beyond fear, let us begin!

As usual, for this to be successful you need to take some measures before we start.

Go to your safe space, switch off all the distractions around you and get comfortable.

Once you are comfortable in your safe space, and after you have removed the sources of distractions such as phones and various notifications, I would like you to start to take some deep breaths and start to imagine once again that you are entering your inner world.

Once you are in your inner world, I will now need you to walk towards your Tree of Life.

Now approach the Tree of Life, look around it, appreciate how it looks and how it feels.

Look carefully, and answer this question: "Have some aspects of your Tree of Life changed?" perhaps the ground seems firmer. Perhaps there are more leaves on the branches. What happened to your Tree of Life?

As usual, just look around the Tree trunk to find the entry point which will lead you back to the room with the green door.

This entry point may differ from the previous one you used, and that is also OK.

Once you gained entry to the Tree of Life, please look around and go to the room with the green door where your Heart lamp lies.

Open the door and enter the room with your green lamp, spend a few moments in the light of your lamp; this is where the energy of your Chakra comes from.

Now pick up your lamp and look around the room: you should be able to see the pink door which guards the secrets of self-love and you should be able to see the other door as well, the door that yesterday was dark and menacing.

More often than not, the colour of that door will have changed since yesterday.

Perhaps it's less dark and ominous, perhaps it is just less scary.

Armed with your Green Chakra lamp, be brave once again and step inside the space that lies beyond that door.

As you enter into this new space, I would like you to look around and perceive the differences that you can spot compared to what you could see yesterday.

Your goal for today is to find the flame of universal love; the flame that holds the love of the universe, nature or god, depending on your spiritual beliefs.

Today you will fully regenerate your lamp with the power of the universal flame. For you to do so though you need to walk back to the place where you met your adversary yesterday.

If everything went according to plan, you should be able to see only one remaining chair and nothing else.

If this is the case, you can proceed with your mission and skip the next section.

If the person is still around: instructions

In some rare occasions though, you may still be able to see a shadow of the person you forgave yesterday.

It will look like a ghostly appearance of that person, not completely formed, with dull colours and translucent.

If this is what you are experiencing, I will need you to completely release this person once again.

Approach the chair one more time, sit and face that person.

As you will be able to feel, this shadowy figure holds much less weight than the actual person that you met yesterday. This is because the majority of the work was done yesterday and today you will need to simply use a little bit of extra forgiveness to seal the deal once and for all.

As you stand in front of the shadow of the person, hold your Heart lamp in your left hand this time.

Focus and think about a time in your life where you felt plenty of love in your Heart. It could be during a beautiful date with a person you loved, it could be for a gorgeous pet or simply the strong love that comes from daily meditations.

Just fill your Heart with love and see the flame of your lamp becoming brighter and stronger.

Once your Heart is filled with love, take the final step and put the lamp in front of the figure and as you do so say these words:

"Love can heal any wound, you are forgiven and it is time to go."

You won't need to repeat this, your Heart just wanted a confirmation of your decisions and now that you have given it one, the bright flame of the lamp will dispel that shadowy figure once and for all.

Once this is achieved, you are free to proceed!

The light at the end of the tunnel

You can now proceed and reap the rewards of your commitment!

Proceed into the space around and let your Heart lamp guide you, this lamp is fuelled by love and it knows perfectly how to get back to its creator, the universal flame.

Walk around until you are able to see from a distance a strong green flame which burns brightly and bravely.

That is the flame where the love of the universe comes from, approach this green flame and feel its beneficial presence upon you.

As you get closer and closer, fill your Heart with it, let it sink deeper into your body, into your mind and your soul.

Feel the gentle frequency of the vibration of the universal love, let it heal your wounds from the past.

Remember that love can heal ANYTHING, just stay there for a few moments.

Once you are ready, I will need you to be brave one more time: look at the flame and while holding your lamp, walk inside the flame and just stay there.

The heat of the flame is gentle, forgiving and caring. It may remind you of when you were still in the womb, protected, safe.

Stay inside the flame of the universal love and look at your lamp.

See how it starts to mend itself, any damage, any rust or dirt will disappear, engulfed by the flame of love of the universe.

As your lamp becomes new, your Heart Chakra becomes new, any damage, any block will just disappear, devoured by the flame.

Stay inside there for a few more moments and let the lamp become completely new and repaired.

Your lamp is now becoming once again *Anahata,* and this time the meaning of it is "Unhurt".

Your Heart Chakra is becoming once again unhurt, like the Heart of a child before knowing the meaning of rejection.

Bask in this power for a while more and when you are ready conclude the practice and get back to your life.

Before you close the book though, I would ask you to read the appendix to this chapter as it will have the instructions for tomorrow's practice.

Appendix to the third journey

Tomorrow will be a special day for you, there will not be a meditation practice tomorrow, but it will still be a special day.

Tomorrow it will be the day you will dedicate to the shower of love.

I will give you clear instructions about what you need to do in a moment, for now I would simply like you to think of tomorrow as a day where you will try your best to do and experience things from a position of love for yourself.

If you remember at the beginning of the practice, I asked you to start this considering that you needed a day off on the fourth day, right?

Well, this day off will be your shower of love day where you will take great care of yourself and will only take actions based on your Heart's happiness.

Shower yourself with love

In the three previous journeys, you have walked through darkness to find the light at the end of the tunnel and today it is time to pamper yourself. You deserve this.

The whole purpose of today is for you to shower yourself with love, rest and recharge your batteries for your next three challenges.

This is how today is going to work:

1. Today there will be no practice, you are taking a day off just for yourself.
2. You are the focus of today. This means that I would like you to dedicate some time for you and take good care of yourself.
3. Ask yourself, what do I want to do today? This is VASTLY different from what you MUST do. Dig deep, what is it that you desire to do today?
4. After you have an answer to the previous question, please go and do it and really enjoy it.

The focus is on your enjoyment and acting in a way that is joyful and takes care of yourself.

This needs to come from your Heart though, today is the first milestone for your new power of self-love that you will awaken in the next three days.

I know you are busy; I know that you may be thinking that you shouldn't do this because other matters have priority over you.

I know that you feel this way, but I also know that these feelings are ABSOLUTELY incorrect!

Let me explain to you why:

You see, self-love and taking good care of your body and your mind is of paramount importance the more you care for others.

This is a trope that often very caring people experience, they put other people always ahead of themselves, ending up denying their own self-love.

What you need to remember though is that the Green Chakra, the one in charge of you taking care of others is only HALF of your Heart.

There is a second part, your pink Heart and this pink Heart needs to balance the green one for you to be healthy.

And why is being healthy so important, ESPECIALLY if you are very caring person?

Well, the truth is that, if by any chance, you were to get ill and NEEDED to take time for yourself to get better, how could you take care of others?

This is a common problem that a lot of people experience, it is typical of people with strong family values. These kinds of people have a shining Green Chakra that empowers them to take great care of the people around them.

Imagine a good parent taking good care of the children alongside having their own career.

In this scenario, this person is constantly rushing for the needs of others:

- take the kids to school
- meet the teachers for their grades
- go to work and pursue their career goals

- collect the kids and prepare a great meal for the family
- take care of the pets in the house etc etc

As you can clearly see, a scenario like this is pretty common in the West.

There are hundreds of super-parents who have a routine similar to the one just mentioned; these people feel a need to do everything they can to take care of their loved ones, their Green Heart Chakras are so strong!

The problem is that this type of behaviour is unsustainable in the long run.

Let me explain why!

It is a fact of life that True Health can ONLY be achieved when you can balance both aspects of you: your physicality, meaning your body, and your emotional and spiritual side.

It is also a fact that continuously working to take care of others without time for yourself, is detrimental to your health.

As a human being, your body is designed to have two important responses:

- The stress response (which sometimes ends up in a real fight or flight response) that is continuously trigged as you go through the day taking care of tasks. These tasks include working, cleaning, taking care of other people, competitive sports and any kind of mental activity requiring your concentration.

- The relaxation response. This is when you SHOULD break out of the stress response and let your body and your spirit rest. The human body, given the time and proper nutrition, is perfectly adapted to get rid of the stress hormones and bringing your body back to balance. This CANNOT happen, unfortunately, if you are constantly running around taking care of others while disregarding yourself.

This is why the next three practices are so important, plenty of good, caring human beings are taught since childhood to put the needs of others ahead of their own needs.

This is extremely noble, and it MUST be balanced by taking time for yourself and relax.

Trust me on this, if you don't take care of yourself, there will be one day when everything breaks down and you WILL get ill and you WILL NOT be able to help others as your health will be in jeopardy.

Do you want more proof on this?

Ok, let me tell about one of the biggest scientific studies on the topic. This paper is a 2015 study conducted by Professor Jennifer N. Morey and her team (see Morey JN, Boggero IA, Scott AB, Segerstrom SC. Current Directions in Stress and Human Immune Function. *Curr Opin Psychol.* 2015;5:13-17. doi:10.1016/j.copsyc.2015.03.007)

This study found, without the shadow of a doubt, a strong connection between stress and the reduced activity of your immune system.

Increased stress was linked to VERY serious conditions such as rheumatoid arthritis, schizophrenia, clinical depression and even MULTIPLE SCLEROSIS.

Do you realise how serious this is?

How do you expect to be able to take care of your family, your business, your pets, if you are not healthy, if you are suffering from a very serious disease?

It is of paramount importance that you listen to the message of the pink part of your Heart and that you dedicate some time to yourself.

Self-love is really important and you NEED TO accept this now.

The more you love others, the more you want to take care of them, the bigger your (green) Heart is, the more you need to be healthy and take some time off to dedicate it yourself.

So, for the rest of the day, or for how long you feel comfortable doing this, please take some time off to dedicate to yourself.

Take a nice bath, go for a walk, read a book, get a massage.

Anything that feels good for you, let your Heart guide you for today, just relax and be.

If your thoughts of commitment arise, tell them you will listen to them later in the day but for now just take ONE action for yourself, start with one for now and if you can do more than one that is even better.

Answer these questions for me please and once you have, please go out there and shower yourself with love, you deserve it!

What it is that I really want to do for myself today? (nothing is not an option by the way ☺)

....
....
....
....
....
....
....
....

What is the ONE action that I WILL do for myself today?

....
....
....
....
....
....
....
....

Journey 4
The discovery of the pink lamp

Welcome to the first of the three days of practice to activate and balance the pink part of your Heart Chakra.

These three days of practice are going to be very intense and life changing for you, this is especially true if you have never been a self-loving person. I cannot wait to start, but, first of all, the instructions.

By now you should know the drill: I need you to go to your safe place, switch off all the distractions around you, and get comfortable.

Read through the instructions for this journey at least once before attempting it, to ensure that everything will go smoothly, and that you will know what to expect.

Once you are comfortable in your safe place, take some deep breaths and begin to imagine once again that you are entering your inner world.

Once you are in your inner world, I will now need you to start to walk towards your Tree of Life.

Once you are at your Tree of Life, you will have two options: you either enter from the front entrance of the tree trunk and pass through the green door to reach the pink one, or you may also enter from the back of the tree, through a different entry point which will lead you directly to the room with the pink door.

Either one is fine, just select the one which resonates with you the most.

From now on, I will assume you are using the back-entry point.

Once you are inside your inner world I will need you to walk around and look for the door that leads to your Pink Heart Chakra; this door is characterised by a pink door.

Once you have found the door, please do enter the room.

As you enter the room you will be able to see and feel this pink light surround you.

It may feel weak and dim for now if you the kind of person who has always put the needs of others ahead of your own needs; this is also fine as we are here to make the light stronger.

Look around the room until you will be able to find the pink lamp.

Sometimes the lamp is very small, sometimes it cracked or dusty.

Just look around and find yours, what does it look like?

Take a good look: is it damaged? Is it dim? Is it dusty or broken?

Do not judge the lamp on the way it looks now, will change dramatically in the next few days as you take good care of you.

For now, just take the lamp with you and keep exploring the room.

I will need you to find a full figure mirror, the exact same mirror that you found when taking the Chakra test. This is the twin of the mirror of truth that you encountered in the middle world the first time you took the Chakra test.

After you have found the mirror of truth, I will need you to go with your lamp to stand in front of the mirror and see yourself reflected in it.

Do not do anything else, as tomorrow will be the day where this conversation will happen.

For now, just get accustomed to the room, the lamp, the mirror and your image there.

And once you are ready, return upstairs and leave this journey and come back to the physical world.

This closes today's experience, a pretty simple task today, BUT tomorrow it will be intense.

There is a good chance that you will cry when you will have a conversation with yourself; this may be especially true if you have neglected yourself for a long time.

This is absolutely fine, just be prepared and bring tissues. ☺

It would be also a good idea to bring pen and paper as you may want to jot down some of the things you will discover about yourself. Finally, it is crucial that NOTHING will interrupt you during tomorrow's journey; the last thing you need is to cut the emotional journey in half due to a distraction.

Prepare everything ahead of time, so that you will be left in peace during the extraordinary experience of awakening your self-love.

Since we are here, if you are enjoying this book please consider leaving a review on Amazon.

Reviews are incredibly helpful for me and they let other people find the book in an easier way.

Let's close this part now, please take the rest of the day off and I will see you tomorrow!

Journey 5
A conversation with your neglected self

Here we go, halfway through the journeys into the pink aspect of your Heart Chakra, and like the previous experience with the green aspect, the halfway mark is the most challenging one.

Today you will have a conversation with your neglected self, and it will emotional, demanding and ultimately cathartic.

I won't waste too much time with the introduction as we need to start the practice.

As usual, you need to go to your safe place, switch off all the distractions around you, and get comfortable.

Read through the instructions for this journey at least once before attempting it, to ensure that everything will go smoothly, and that you know what to expect.

Once you are comfortable in your safe place, take some deep breaths and begin to imagine once again that you are entering your inner world.

Once you are in your inner world, start to walk towards your Tree of Life.

The tree trunk will contain the entry point to your inner world where the Heart Chakra resides.

Enter the Tree of Life and look around until you will be able to find the room with the pink door where your pink lamp is.

Once you enter the room, I will need you to look around and find your pink lamp.

As usual, the first step is to take a look at the lamp. Has anything changed since you were yesterday?

Take a good look and when ready, hold your lamp with your left hand and proceed to face the mirror.

Remember this is the mirror of truth and this mirror will always show you and tell you nothing but the truth.

As you stand in front of the mirror, face yourself and then greet the image that you see in the mirror.

The image in the mirror is you, but you may look different from how you look in the physical world, this is absolutely fine.

Many people see themselves smaller or younger, sometimes older, allow and accept the image that you perceive now in the mirror as you are here to heal.

After greeting yourself in the mirror, the next stage is for you to thank you other self for being here and listening to you.

Thank the image for its kindness in showing up despite the times you have neglected her.

And now listen or feel and answer these questions, ideally by also taking notes:

What is the image telling you when you thank her?

....

....

....

....

....

Listen carefully as the image has a profound message for you, a message that you should have listened to some time ago, but you did not.

That does not matter anymore though, as you are now here to make amends and peace with your past.

The next question that you will need to ask yourself is this, and please write down the answer:

Are you ready to accept my apologies for neglecting you in the past?

....

....

....

....

....

This time the responses may be subjective, as it depends how much you have neglected taking care of yourself, just note down the answer from the mirror.

If the answer is yes, then proceed with the conversation, if the answer is no you will need to ask another question:

What is the ONE action that you want me to do in the physical world to make amends and peace with you?

....

....

....

....

....

Please note the answer down as this will be something that you will need to execute in the following days.

Once you have noted down the response, the image in the mirror will be ready to forgive you, as long as you perform the requested action in the physical world.

It is now time to have your vision, so move closer to the mirror and sit on the ground and keep your pink lamp in your lap.

Once you are closer to the mirror, look at your image and ask:

Please show me when I hurt you the most.

The vision and the feeling you will get from this situation may be really strong and often leads to tears.

You may see yourself neglecting your health or wellbeing for many different reasons and it is OK now.

You are here to make amends not to judge yourself, accept what has already happened and your love will heal this deep wound.

For now, just look and let your other self show you what is the source of that strong pain.

Let it in, accept it and finally appreciate her gift of showing you the truth as the truth will make you free.

Please now take a note of what you saw, I know it may be hard and intense, but I need you to focus now. Please do write down your vision and your perception of the situation.

What did I see/feel?

....

....

....

....

....

What have I learnt about the experience and myself?

....

....

....

....

....

And finally after you have raised your awareness regarding this situation, it is now time for you to be brave and tell your image that you thank it for its honesty and that you will do your best to make amends tomorrow.

Now we need to close this practice here and you shall close the practice with love, plenty of true, beautiful love.

Hold your lamp in your hand and walk inside the mirror, you will see that the glass is like liquid mercury and it allows you to walk inside and once you are inside, while holding the lamp with you, go close to your other self and simply hug her.

Stay there hugging your other self for as much as you need. This is a love hug, this is a healing hug that is cancelling the wounds of the past with the power of your Pink Chakra.

Let the pink flame embrace you both, reassure your other self, hold her tight and finish the meditation inside the mirror, loving your other self and holding her tight.

If possible try to sleep for the next few minutes, it is well deserved, also please do note down any dream that you may experience between now and your awakening tomorrow morning.

Journey 6
Love can heal all wounds

I am sure yesterday was a pretty intense situation and you may have questions or need some guidance, if you do please drop a request to join my *"Chakras Explained with Nick Zanetti"* private group on Facebook where I can give you further guidance, or should you prefer to do this experience in a guided journey with me on Skype, just drop an email to info@nicolazanetti.org and we can take it from there.

It is now time to resume your practice. As usual, you need to go to your safe place, switch off all the distractions around you, and get comfortable.

Read through the instructions for this journey at least once before attempting it, to ensure that everything will go smoothly, and that you know what to expect.

Once you are comfortable in your safe place, take some deep breaths and begin to imagine once again that you are entering your inner world.

At the end of yesterday's journey, you closed your visualisation with you inside the mirror of truth hugging your other self.

This is where the journey will restart today.

As you slowly awaken in your inner world, you can find yourself there once again.

You are holding your Pink Chakra lamp and you are hugging the version of yourself that was in the mirror.

Today you will be able to see that this version of you is now feeling better than before.

This is because you have started the process of healing through the amends and the gift of self-love.

It is now time to take things to the next stage, hold the pink lamp in your hand and take your other self's hand with your right hand, so both of you can walk out of the mirror, back to the room where the pink lamp was.

Guide your reflection through the pink room to the green door. This green door is around here somewhere, just look around and you will be able to find it.

Once it has been found, open the door and while still holding your pink lamp and the hand of your other self, reach the green room and approach your green lamp.

Entering the room will make your Heart buzz with joy, this lamp has already been strongly empowered with the flame of universal love and its light and strength are remarkable but gentle.

Once in the room you will notice something: your other self is confused by this green light.

Depending on how much you have neglected yourself in the past, your other self will be either confused or wondering what this green light actually is.

This green light is something new if you haven't spent lots of time showering yourself with love and this is absolutely fine.

Now take the green lamp in your right hand and the pink one in the left hand, and as you do so please sit on the ground facing your other self.

You see, if you are here reading this book right now I am very confident that destiny, or the universe if you will brought you to this moment in time and space to achieve something incredible.

You may have been a person who has helped a lot of other living beings around you and you may not have spent enough time for yourself.

Now we will change that once and for all.

Remember, the green lamp contains the energy of Green Heart Chakra, this energy comes from the infinite love of the universe and it is now time, perhaps for the first time in your life to turn this beautiful green flame towards your other self.

I will need you to pour your Heart into this practice, feel you Heart filling itself with love and become lighter and lighter as the flame in lamp becomes warmer and warmer.

Let this warm, loving feeling embrace your other self, let this love heal all of her wounds, no matter where they are in time or space.

Universal love knows no boundaries and you are now using your great capacity of loving others and being altruistic towards your neglected self.

As you do so you will see your other self relaxing and becoming more and more translucent.

Love is healing your wounds of the past and there is no need to hold on to any bad thoughts that you may have had.

As your neglected self starts to become more and more translucent, I will need you to face her, look into her eyes and with profound conviction and elation just say:

I love you! I love you from the bottom of my Heart.

As you do so, picture your other self smiling and accepting what you are saying, completely forgiving you and removing any trace of division between you two.

Say these words twice more for me:

I love you! I love you from the bottom of my Heart.

I love you! I love you from the bottom of my Heart.

Notice how your other self is now finally starting to disappear and as the green light grows stronger, bid farewell to your neglected self by saying the words one more time:

I love you! I love you from the bottom of my Heart.

As you finish pronouncing the words, look at your other self disappearing with a smile and feel deep in your Heart that you are forgiven, that your love now has healed the wounds of your past and that you are now forgiven and ready to move to the next stage of your life.

Look at the green lamp and notice that something really strange is happening: as your green light becomes a bit dimmer, your pink light becomes a bit stronger and now the lamps hold the same intensity of light.

Both the aspects of your Heart Chakras are starting to align and clear themselves and tomorrow we will complete the practice by creating true balance between both aspects of your Heart Chakra.

That is for tomorrow though, you can rest now.

Please take a few moments for yourself and feel proud of what you have achieved, you have faced your inner fears and shame and with the power of love you are balancing the flow of Ki in your body and your soul.

Time to relax and I will see you tomorrow.

Journey seven
Achieving perfect balance between the two aspects of your Heart

Here we are, final journey of this book, this is where we will finally find the balance between the two aspects of your Heart and help you to find the same equilibrium in other aspects of your life.

As I have previously mentioned, the Heart Chakra is such an important element of the practice of inner journeying.

This is because most people's path crosses with mine in a moment where they are hurt, or vulnerable and they need to find something to balance themselves and the pure love that comes from the Heart is the best medicine there is for that.

Unfortunately, it is also quite common for people who like to learn more about spirituality to be greener oriented than pink oriented. This means being more in touch with their side who helps and cherishes others and less with the side who loves themselves.

I see this all the time when I teach nutrition in college, every year there around 300 new people coming to college and when I speak to most of them I can clearly see a strong Green Heart Chakra, the Heart of a true healer and that is great for the career they have chosen. At the same time, when I discuss taking care of oneself and having time for oneself, I can also clearly see that a lot of people simply do not have that luxury, or think that they don't deserve that.

This will change at the end of today's journey and if you will weekly revisit what we do today, this balance will stay with you for good!

With the introduction cleared, it is now time to begin!

As usual, I need you to go to your safe place, switch off all the distractions around you, and get comfortable.

Read through the instructions for this journey at least once before attempting it, to ensure that everything will go smoothly, and that you know what to expect. Also for this journey it would be ideal if you could complete the exercises before you actually do the whole experience.

Ideally you want to read through the chapter and complete the exercises BEFORE you actually take the journey with focus and attention. The exercises are extremely important in this chapter, so please listen to these instructions as they can change things forever.

Once you are comfortable in your safe place, take some deep breaths and begin to imagine once again that you are entering your inner world.

Once you are in your inner world, start to walk towards your Tree of Life.

Find the entry point to reach one of the two rooms, either the pink or the green, whichever one you fancy: it doesn't really matter as we will use both.

Travel inside the Tree of Life and find the room which contains the green lamp, the green aspect of your Heart Chakra and the room with the pink lamp which contains the pink lamp aspect of your Heart.

Once you are inside those rooms, find and collect both of the lamps.

You are now holding your green lamp and your pink one, perfect!

Now I will need you to look up at the ceiling, but you will see that the ceiling is not actually there and you can see above you the big arms of a balance scale.

Yes! That's right, the two rooms hosting the two aspects of your Heart are actually the two plates of a giant balance scale, isn't that amazing?

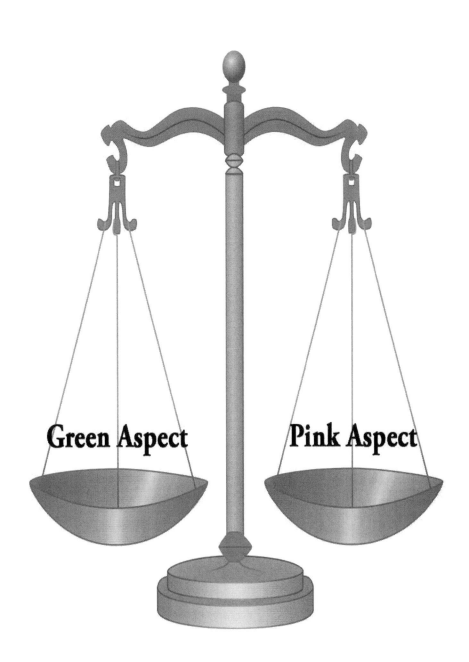

Green Aspect

Pink Aspect

Now look around carefully and notice where the plates are tilted towards.

Is the equilibrium of your Heart Chakra tilted towards the green aspect, is it towards the pink one?

Or are they PERFECTLY balanced?

Please take a good look, or even walk around to feel if there is an incline between the two rooms and once you are sure please write down what you have noticed.

My Heart balance is tilted more towards:

....

....

....

....

....

Excellent, now that you have found where you stand in the grand scheme of things, we can start the balancing aspect of this journey.

Let us begin with the green room: investigate the green room until you find a green X on the ground.

That X is the place of balance of the green plate. Once you have found it, please place the green lamp on the X and you will see that it fits perfectly and locks itself there.

Now back to the pink room, once again look around until you see a pink X on the ground.

That is the place where you will need to place your pink lamp, as you do so you will see that lamp locks in place.

Now you have both lamps perfectly locked at the centre of balance of each of the plates, and you also know which of the two aspects of your Heart Chakra is dominant on the other.

Let us now start to bring everything back towards the real equilibrium.

Please go and sit on the ground where the door between the green and the pink room is.

Sit there and find your perfect balance, the left side of your body needs to be in the pink room whereas the right side of your body needs to be in the green room.

Sit there and focus for a moment and in the physical world I will need you to put your hands on your Heart.

Stay there for a moment and feel your Heart, feel it beating.

Your Heart is the source of life, with its beating it brings oxygen and energy all around your body, feeding your body and sustaining you.

Since you in your mother's womb, your Heart has been there for you, beating, pumping, keeping you alive.

Your Heart is your best friend, your biggest fan and it constantly works for you without taking a break.

Feel your chest expanding as you breath and feel your Heart beating and as you do so, you will start to feel the frequency of vibration of your Heart.

Your Heart has always been there for you and it is now time for you to give back.

As you hold your hands on your Heart, thank your Heart for being there for you.

Say with me please:

Thank you
Thank you
Thank you
And one more time
Thank you

The Heart doesn't get enough credit for its incredible job in keeping you alive and supporting you but today we are changing that.

Your Heart has always been there for you and it has helped you experience some of the most amazing moments of your life, and some of the darkest ones.

And that is also OK!

Spend a few moments with your Heart and think about three things you are grateful for.

The first thing I am grateful for is:

....

....

....

....

....

The second thing I am grateful for is:

....

....

....

....

....

The third thing I am grateful for is:

....

....

....

....

....

....

Once you have these three things in your mind, it is now time to pour them into your Heart.

Think about the first thing that you are grateful for, feel it, imagine it, see it, make it real in your mind and let it vibrate with the frequency of your Heart.

Feel your Heart accepting this gratitude, feel your Heart filling up with this gratitude.

You are giving back to an old friend, someone who always had your back and kept you alive no matter how hard you may have tried to damage your life.

You are here, you are alive, and your Heart is still beating and nurturing you.

Be grateful for that, accept that your life has a profound meaning and that the particular frequency of your Heart is just yours, no one has the same frequency as you and the universe knows that.

Now go to the second reason why you are grateful, once again imagine it, feel it and once it's clear in your mind pour it in your Heart.

Let that gratitude clear your Heart Chakra and balance it.

This gratitude is a strong gift that is helping you and healing you right now.

Give this gratitude back to your oldest friend, your Heart. Give the gratitude back and feel your Heart healing. No matter how deep a wound it had , it is now healing, love is the strongest medicine there is!

And now go to your third reason to be grateful, let it grow in your mind and once it is clear, pour it in your Heart and fill your Heart with gratitude.

As you do so, feel your Heart expanding and warming up; the gratitude is healing you, balancing everything that needs balance.

Trust the gratitude, trust the universal love and more importantly trust your Heart completely and once you have done so, please look around and notice something incredible.

The two plates of the balance scale are now perfectly aligned, your gratitude was capable of healing and balancing both aspects of your Heart.

Now you can go back to your garden and conclude the experience of the day, one last thing though: please leave the door between the green and the pink room open.

Now come back to the physical world and once you have, take a good rest for at least 15 minutes, you clearly deserve that and when you are ready, please keep reading as I have a couple of things to say in the appendix to this journey.

I will see you soon.

Appendix to the seventh journey

OK, here we are!

First of all, welcome back and let me tell you how proud I am of you for being here after having taken the time to do 7 days of practice.

This is an incredible achievement and it shows the type of person you have decided to become, please take a moment to congratulate yourself because you have been amazing!

Now back to the appendix of the chapter: you see, there is something that I need to clarify here and that is really important for you to understand.

You have just done this inner journey to balance the two aspects of your Heart Chakra, and as it stands they have found the perfect equilibrium between them.

This situation will be stable for a few days, but then it's possible that life will get into the way. Perhaps you will once again put the needs of others ahead of your self-love, perhaps someone will say something nasty about you, or perhaps habits will go back to the way they were.

All of this is fine, as long as you revert the change back to balance once you realise that the rooms are once again misaligned.

So, probably once per week I would strongly suggest you repeat this experience, this last journey and through the power of gratitude rebalance the two aspects of your Heart.

An important notice here: remember to change the things you are grateful for every now and then.

The reason for that is that we, sometimes, grow accustomed to the gratitude exercise and the same reason to be grateful doesn't hold the same strength anymore.

Remember, during the exercise you want to create an incredibly powerful feeling of gratitude, because that strength and energy that you will be feeling, will be the same wavelength which will balance the flow of Ki in your Heart Chakra.

Try to find new powerful reasons to be grateful because they will be the most powerful medicine there is for your Heart Chakra.

Another piece of advice that I would like to give you is the idea of keeping a gratitude journal.

This is a journal where you weekly write down three things you are grateful for and this will keep you in this strong sense of gratitude and abundance, which are in my opinion, the best way to experience the journey of being a human being.

If you need inspiration as an idea on how to structure this gratitude journal, you can find a list of the three things in my workbook *What is Chakra Healing Chakra Info Workbook.*

To close this chapter, I would like to ask you one more time to consider leaving me a review on amazon Then I will conclude by sharing with you the experience of one of my strongest journeys to heal my Heart in the last chapter of the book.

Reviews really support authors and help other people find the books, so if you think that someone else may benefit of my work, please consider leaving a review for the book.

Let us now go to the conclusion and my private journey into my Heart.

Conclusion

Final chapter of the book, what an intense experience.

Even when writing, the simple description of the journeys felt so strong and real to me, and I am sure it felt the same to you.

At this point of the book, you are now an expert on how your Heart Chakra works, you have learnt about its two aspects and we both journeyed together to reclaim your balance and open your Heart Chakra.

I want to close the book with a couple of pieces of advice as they will be important for you in the following week and in the following month.

The first thing that may happen, or has already happened, is your Heart Chakra becoming fully open for a couple of days.

This is something that may happen in the following days or may already have happened.

If this is the case, you will feel a strong sense of love and wonder for essentially anything around you.

Food will taste incredibly good; colours may be become fuller and brighter and you may feel tears of joy coming out of nowhere.

This is OK, the Chakra will slow down in a couple of days, it won't stay like that forever, but as long as it is like that, I guess you can just enjoy the situation and the feeling of oneness with the universe around you.

If you do end up experiencing an open Heart Chakra, keep this memory around deep in your Heart for the rest of your time as a mortal on this planet. This feeling of oneness and interconnectedness with all life, with God, the universe and everything around you will be extremely precious during your last moments as a human on this planet. This memory will always be with you lifting the fear of death as an end and reassuring that your soul, your energy will live on forever, this will be the last gift of your closest friend, your Heart, the final gift of bravery in the face of death.

The second thing that may happen to you, is some sort of a change in your relationships, be it in romantic relationships or friendships.

See, a balanced Heart is incredibly attractive and its pure, glowing energy may attract other spiritual people into your life, when that happens, just trust your Heart and go with the flow.

Even if you were really hurt in the past, and even if you felt that loving someone deeply is now beyond your possibility, with your newfound Heart you will see that is not only possible but probable.

Finally, if you have not yet met your Twin Flame, or if you have lost your Twin Flame, a healthy Heart is the best way to meet your other half.

There is nothing more attractive to your Soul Mate than a healthy, glowing and balanced Heart.

So, be prepared for when that happens ☺

This is the end of the book and in the final bonus chapter I will share with you one of my advanced journeys and you will see what happened to me during one of the darkest moments of my life and how journeys changed that for good.

There is nothing more powerful than the power of love to achieve true healing, and I can tell you this from a therapist perspective of someone who has worked, in the course of [how many?] years, with hundreds of different clients.

It didn't matter how much I was changing their diets, recommending supplements and lifestyle changes, if they weren't loving themselves, those scientific solutions were short-lived and true health was impossible to achieve.

Let me remind you one last time that this book is designed to be a PRACTICAL journey into the balance and opening of the Heart Chakra.

Its sole purpose is to guide you and teach you with PRACTICALITY what needs to be done to balance your Heart, so if by any chance, you have just read the book without taking the time to do the practice, I implore you to go back and do it.

Following the practice, exactly as it is instructed, is the way to go!

All the knowledge of the world about your Chakras will not change anything if you do not practice, this is especially true for the Heart Chakra as this particular Chakra is empowered by feeling rather studying and knowing.

This closes the book, remember to live strong, live with passion at the best of your abilities.

Let your Heart guide you, be brave and do the things that scare you because beyond that fear you can find the secret of true love and this true love will change everything for you!

London 23/6/2020

Advanced journeying: Healing the "Slash in the Soul"

What I am about to share with you is an example of advanced journey.

I am including this in the book as the practice of journeying is more of an art than it is a science.

See, sometimes journeys take a direction that is different from what you would expect. This is the reason for me being so specific in the instructions of the guided journeys and using specific language patterns to make everything homogenous for anybody.

The truth of the matter though, is that the more you journey, the more differences you will find compared to the first time and your inner world will change accordingly to the new flow of Ki through your Chakras.

The example of the journey that I am about to share with you, shows clearly that this practice is like a well-designed film: full of twists and turns.

So, should you decide that you need direct guidance for your practice and have me as your coach during your journeys, you can book an online session with me by sending an email at info@nicolazanetti.org

Also, if you unsure about something that is happening to you during the journeys please consider joining our private Facebook group called *Chakras Explained with Nick Zanetti.*

Now, that I have covered all the basics I am ready to share my story and the journey that helped me to balance the deepest damage to my Heart Chakra.

I strongly suggest you use a specific Heart Chakra musical video as you read the rest of the story as it will really help you get in touch with my ordeal.

The YouTube video I am suggesting to you is from a channel called Meditative Mind and the title of the video is extremely powerful Heart Chakra opening vibrations (1 hour version) and you can find it here

Now turn your music on and let me give you the context of the situation.

Back in 2003 I was in a very intense long-distance relationship with an Italian girl; we were both young and naïve but, in my Heart, I thought she was the One!

For the first three months of our relationship, everything was going perfectly, we had perfect romantic and sexual harmony and it was so great.

Unfortunately, at the end of this quick honeymoon period things started to go downhill, mostly because my roots were weak, and I often felt very jealous.

This jealousy started to push her away, deep in my soul I was afraid that the long-distance would be detrimental and she would end up cheating on me. And by now, you know how the universe works, as you think, so you attract.

During those first weeks of relationship issues, she started to act more distant than before. She was slower to text me back, sometimes she didn't pick up the phone etc.

This change in her behaviour, which in the ultimate analysis was caused by my jealousy, made me very needy and clingy.

This was obviously not good for the relationship as it pushed her even further away.

The fear of losing her became a terror and I was spending so much time waiting for the big moment when she would break up with me.

Each text I was receiving was not welcome anymore but I was opening it with a heavy Heart expecting that text to be the one where she was breaking up with me.

I was pouring this fear into the universe more and more and, at the same time, my behaviour was becoming less and less attractive with me being jealous and annoying for literally no reason.

The reality is that when you put so much effort into imagining something, in the end you will make it real and hey presto! Someone came along and started going out with her.

It took us around one month to acknowledge what was really going on and finally break up.

During that time, I had become so needy that the poor girl didn't know how to break up with me anymore. I was constantly reminding her she was my life and I couldn't live without her.

At the end, during my last visit to her house I ended up picking up a conversation she was having over the phone and realised she had another man in her life.

As I said before, my roots were very weak at the time, I had never heard about self-improvement, I didn't have the means to process what was happening to me and I wasn't really understanding what was going on.

I ended up doing something stupid: I was associating how much pain I was feeling with how much love I still had for her.

So, every day of life was a race to try and cause myself more pain by thinking about all the good moments with her, being stuck in the past and refusing to move over only to prove to myself that she was still the love of my life, my Twin Flame.

171

The problem was that the more I was evoking that pain, the darker my mood went and the less of a prospective in the future I could see.

It really went downhill to the point where I really didn't even want to leave my bed anymore and I had contemplated, several times, the idea of taking my life.

During that period of pain and despair, I used to watch a popular Italian night-time talk show to try and counter my sleepless nights.

It was during one of the episodes of the show that I had heard a concept which was clearly describing what I was experiencing at the time. There was an author who was being interviewed at the time, and she was describing a concept in her book: the idea that when someone is emotionally badly hurt, the soul gets also damaged and she called that "The slash in the soul".

That concept was so in touch with what I was feeling since it was like there was a hole deep in my chest, a hole full of nothingness.

Luckily for me things started to get better and I was able to survive that period and get back into balance.

I survived that event, but that didn't mean that I was actually back in balance! For many years in fact, until the journey I am about to share with you, I had lost the capacity of deeply loving someone.

I could get a crush yes, but I couldn't really go deep as I felt that "the slash in the soul" was still there and I was terrified to repeat that dreadful experience, so it was safer for me not to get emotionally involved.

As you can expect at this point of a book on the Heart Chakra, that is really detrimental to the health of your energy centre.

Flash forward to 2007 when I started my journey into self-development with various books, among them Hawaiian Magic by Clark Wilkerson.

This was the first book that taught me the idea of changing things into your Inner World to balance your life and helped me to develop my own way of working with the flow of Ki in the body that you are reading in this series of books.

Armed with the understanding that I had from that book, I had the journey that I am about to share with you to heal "the Slash in the Soul".

Now without further ado, let me show what had happened during that incredible journey to heal my damaged Heart.

"As I close my eyes, I enter my inner world, it took me weeks before finally deciding to do this journey.

What I will face today has been a terrible source of pain and despair for me for many years, I am shaken, and I am not sure if I want to follow through with this.

I guess this is normal though, it is the destiny of humanity to face our inner demons and so I keep going.

Entering my inner world, I am in front of the house in Italy where I was born. I know that my Tree of Life lies just down the road and so I start walking.

The air is warm and stale, nobody is around, and everything is silent.

As I approach the Tree, I can see it, it is a giant oak tree lying there in front of the of the oldest mansion of the town.

My father told me that this tree was planted before world war one, this makes it more than 90 years old!

I am now facing the my entry point to the tree and I am still on edge, the temperature is now hot, the air is still and I realise for the first time that there seems to be no sign of life around me, nothing at all.

This is like being in a bubble where time has stopped, waiting for a major showdown.

I guess this could be the way two gunmen were feeling prior to their death duel at noon.

I am afraid to enter the tree, I would like to just open my eyes and get it over with, but if I do I will probably sabotage my current relationship like I did until now, so I push through.

I enter the Tree of Life and walk towards the place my Heart Chakra lamp lies.

There it lies waiting for me hanging from the ceiling of a dark room. Its green light is dim and the lamp itself is a complete mess: dull, dusty and with a large slash in the metal cover.

The slash is deep and as I investigate it, I can see darkness pouring from it. It is "the slash in the soul" all right.

I take my Heart lamp and I now ask myself what's next.

My intuition tells me that to repair the lamp so I need to find to find a forge and as I think about the forge I feel once again on edge.

To access the forge, I will need to pass through an adversary, and this will be the toughest and scariest of my adversaries yet.

At this point I want to push through though and get it over with. It has been such a long time since I felt I could let go and feel safe in a romantic relationship, I need to take this chance despite the fear and the apprehension that I am currently feeling.

So, I leave the room and start to walk down a path, this is a path that leads to a field, the same field that faces the elementary school in my hometown.

I know where the forge is now: at the centre of the field there is a metal shack where agricultural tools are kept, the forge is in there.

As I start to approach the shack, the temperature rises even more, now it really hot and humid like the terrible summer of 2003 when the events unfolded. I guess it makes sense.

Suddenly I start to hear an odd noise, like a gigantic hornet buzzing in my hear. I look up towards the sky and see something coming from the sky. It looks like a meteor and it is aiming directly for the field I am in.

The enemy is coming and as it does so, everything goes even staler and the atmosphere becomes more humid than if we were in a tropical forest, and the light is dimming like it was an eclipse.

The meteor keeps falling and now I can hear the roaring thunder of a gigantic waterfall in my hears, it is getting closer and closer and when it strikes the ground, the explosion leaves me dazed and knocked down.

I step back up and look around, the field is now black with the ashes from the meteor fall, but the *shack still stands untouched and as I look towards the shack I see a shadowy figure enter the shack.*

The enemy is there waiting for me, I take a few more steps and then I am very close to the shack and I start to hear a low and angry growl coming from the shack.

The door is open and I can see a flame inside, I guess it's the forge, but there is plenty of darkness still and the growl is growing stronger.

From the darkness I finally see the source of the noise, I can see a pair of burning yellow eyes piercing the darkness and looking directly into my soul.

The adversary has taken the shape of an angry dog, I can see it leaving the shack and walking towards me.

It is a nightmarish version of a German shepherd.

I now know why I am seeing this shape: several years ago when I was 6 or 7 years old during a hot summer day I was walking back home from the youth centre, as I was approaching this same field I saw a dog in the field and as the dog saw me it started to charge me.

I was watching this large dog charging at me and I was feeling completely impotent, I was frozen, and I couldn't move, and the dog was coming and coming.

True blue terror had enveloped me, and I was shaking and then a whistle came!

The owner of the dog whistled, and the dog stopped in its track no more than two meters away from me.

I guess it makes sense that the adversary is something like what I am seeing right now.

I need to get inside and put my lamp into the forge to mend it, but the dog is in my way.

Its fangs are bare, and it is still growling. I try to take a step towards the shack but the dogs bolts and barks showing me its fangs even more.

This is not the right move.

I am frozen in time once again; I feel the same way I felt as a child and then I realise something: I am not a child anymore!

I look at my hands, and legs and feet and these are body parts of an adult.

As I realise this my green lamp starts to burn slightly brighter and now, I understand the meaning of this journey and the enemy.

Healing your Heart requires bravery, love requires bravery!

This is because nothing is guaranteed when it comes to love, and relationship and this unpredictability can freeze yourself in time if you do not face it.

The wounds from the past are strong but facing them is the only way out.

This reminds me of a book that I read about panic attacks; its main message was "the only way out is through it."

So, forward I go regardless of the growls, the fangs and the crazy reactions of the dog.

And as I keep walking towards the entrance, I can see the dog becoming smaller and smaller.

It is still trying to act tough, but now as it is the size of a chihuahua it is certainly not threatening any longer.

I finally enter the shack and reach the forge and I look at "the slash in the soul" one last time. The darkness is still there, it originated by the depression of that period and the dark thoughts that almost cost me my life, but it is now time to let go of all of this.

I put the lamp into the forge, and I have a strong feeling that I will need to come back here in the next three days to rekindle the flame of the forge.

This is something I can do and as I leave the lamp mending itself into the forge, I start to float and drift back to the physical world.

Are you looking for more titles from Nick Zanetti?

This is his <u>author page</u>

In the same series these books are already available:

- What is Chakra healing: Chakra info and how to open your Chakras with guided inner journeys (Book Zero)
- What is Chakra healing Chakra info workbook

Printed in Great Britain
by Amazon